W9-BQS-637

Texas A&M University
College Station, Texas

Written by Ashley Marshall

Edited by Kimberly Moore and Jon Skindzier

Layout by Adam Burns

*Additional contributions by Omid Gohari,
Christina Koshzow, Chris Mason, Joey Rahimi,
and Luke Skurman*

COLLEGE PROWLER

ISBN # 1-4274-0145-4
ISSN # 1552-0765
© Copyright 2005 College Prowler
All Rights Reserved
Printed in the U.S.A.
www.collegeprowler.com

Last updated 5/30/06

Special thanks to: Babs Carryer, Andy Hannah, LaunchCyte, Tim O'Brien, Bob Sehlinger, Thomas Emerson, Andrew Skurman, Barbara Skurman, Bert Mann, Dave Lehman, Daniel Fayock, Chris Babyak, The Donald H. Jones Center for Entrepreneurship, Terry Slease, Jerry McGinnis, Bill Ecenberger, McGinty, Kyle Russell, Jacque Zaremba, Larry Winderbaum, Paul Kelly, Roland Allen, Jon Reider, Team Evankovich, Lauren Varacalli, Abu Noaman, Mark Exler, Daniel Steinmeyer, Jared Cohon, Gabriela Oates, David Koegler, and Glen Meakem.

Bounce-Back Team: Lindsay Moffett, Sara Duran, Bryan Osborne.

College Prowler®
5001 Baum Blvd.
Suite 750
Pittsburgh, PA 15213

Phone: 1-800-290-2682
Fax: 1-800-772-4972
E-mail: info@collegeprowler.com
Web Site: www.collegeprowler.com

Welcome to College Prowler®

During the writing of College Prowler's guidebooks, we felt it was critical that our content was unbiased and unaffiliated with any college or university. We think it's important that our readers get honest information and a realistic impression of the student opinions on any campus—that's why if any aspect of a particular school is terrible, we (unlike a campus brochure) intend to publish it. While we do keep an eye out for the occasional extremist—the cheerleader or the cynic—we take pride in letting the students tell it like it is. We strive to create a book that's as representative as possible of each particular campus. Our books cover both the good and the bad, and whether the survey responses point to recurring trends or a variation in opinion, these sentiments are directly and proportionally expressed through our guides.

College Prowler guidebooks are in the hands of students throughout the entire process of their creation. Because you can't make student-written guides without the students, we have students at each campus who help write, randomly survey their peers, edit, layout, and perform accuracy checks on every book that we publish. From the very beginning, student writers gather the most up-to-date stats, facts, and inside information on their colleges. They fill each section with student quotes and summarize the findings in editorial reviews. In addition, each school receives a collection of letter grades (A through F) that reflect student opinion and help to represent contentment, prominence, or satisfaction for each of our 20 specific categories. Just as in grade school, the higher the mark the more content, more prominent, or more satisfied the students are with the particular category.

Once a book is written, additional students serve as editors and check for accuracy even more extensively. Our bounce-back team—a group of randomly selected students who have no involvement with the project—are asked to read over the material in order to help ensure that the book accurately expresses every aspect of the university and its students. This same process is applied to the 200-plus schools College Prowler currently covers. Each book is the result of endless student contributions, hundreds of pages of research and writing, and countless hours of hard work. All of this has led to the creation of a student information network that stretches across the nation to every school that we cover. It's no easy accomplishment, but it's the reason that our guides are such a great resource.

When reading our books and looking at our grades, keep in mind that every college is different and that the students who make up each school are not uniform—as a result, it is important to assess schools on a case-by-case basis. Because it's impossible to summarize an entire school with a single number or description, each book provides a dialogue, not a decision, that's made up of 20 different topics and hundreds of student quotes. In the end, we hope that this guide will serve as a valuable tool in your college selection process. Enjoy!

OMID GOHARI ○ CHRISTINA KOSHZOW ○ CHRIS MASON ○ JOEY RAHIMI ○ LUKE SKURMAN ○
The College Prowler Team

TEXAS A&M UNIVERSITY
Table of Contents

Introduction from the Author

Four years ago, I posted names of colleges on a dartboard and attempted to make my decision by the random throw of a dart. If you are thinking of becoming an Aggie, this guide will offer you what some Texas A&M students have to say; at the very least, it will make your college decision-making process a little more logical than mine was.

The presence of the uniformed Corps of Cadets still ties us to the past and supports their claim that they are the keepers of tradition. There is a train running through the middle of campus that has ties to the formation of the city of College Station, which can also be used as an excuse for getting to class late. Tradition is still a part of daily life here at A&M.

The week after the terrorist attacks of September 11th, Texas A&M students organized a Red, White and Blue-Out, where instead of wearing our school color, maroon, everyone in the stadium, including the alumni side, wore the colors of the flag. The first decks wore blue, the middle wore white, and the third wore red. Walking up the ramp to Kyle Field, I caught a glimpse of 83,000 people joining together to support America, and the sight was completely overwhelming. No other school could have organized and supported this gesture on such short notice, and this filled me with tremendous honor and a sobering pride at A&M. Witnessing all of this during my freshman year gave me a heartwarming feeling: I knew this was the school for me.

It's difficult to see the entire picture of Texas A&M through cold stats and boring facts, but after reading this guide, you'll see just how different it is from any other campus in America. Pay attention, because the following pages could very well be the next best thing to living on campus yourself. Hopefully, all the opinions in this book will give you a better picture of the real A&M.

Ashley Marshall, Author
Texas A&M University

By the Numbers

General Information

Texas A&M University
College Station, TX
77843

Control:
Public

Academic Calendar:
Semester

Religious Affiliation:
None

Founded:
1876

Web Site:
www.tamu.edu

Main Phone:
(979) 845-3211

Admissions Phone:
(979) 845-3741

Student Body

**Full-Time
Undergraduates:**
32,374

**Part-Time
Undergraduates:**
3,358

**Total Male
Undergraduates:**
18,163

**Total Female
Undergraduates:**
17,569

Admissions

Overall Acceptance Rate:
72%

Total Applicants:
17,324

Total Acceptances:
12,426

Freshman Enrollment:
7,068

Yield (% of admitted students who actually enroll):
57%

Early Decision Available?
Yes

Early Action Available?
No

Early Decision Deadline:
December 1

Regular Decision Deadline:
February 15

Regular Decision Notification:
late March

Must-Reply-By Date:
May 1

Applicants Placed on Waiting List:
1,778

Applicants Accepted from Waiting List:
770

Students Enrolled from Waiting List:
739

Transfer Applications Received:
3,050

Transfer Applications Accepted:
1,904

Transfer Students Enrolled:
1,526

Transfer Application Acceptance Rate:
62%

Common Application Accepted?
Yes

Supplemental Forms?
No

Admissions E-Mail:
admissions@tamu.edu

Admissions Web Site:
www.tamu.edu/admissions

SAT I or ACT Required?
Either

**First-Year Students
Submitting SAT Scores:**
75%

**SAT I Range
(25th–75th Percentile):**
1070–1300

**SAT I Verbal Range
(25th–75th Percentile):**
520–640

**SAT I Math Range
(25th–75th Percentile):**
550–660

Retention Rate:
88%

**Top 10% of
High School Class:**
53%

Application Fee:
$50

Financial Information

Full-Time Tuition:
$5,955 in-state
$13,695 out-of-state

Room and Board:
$6,890

Books and Supplies:
$1,186

Average Need-Based:
$8,800

**Students Who Applied
for Financial Aid:**
64%

Students Who Received Aid:
36%

Financial Aid Forms Deadline:
April 1

Financial Aid Phone:
(979) 845-3917

Financial Aid E-Mail:
financialaid@tamu.edu

Financial Aid Web Site:
http://financialaid.tamu.edu

Academics

The Lowdown On...
Academics

Degrees Awarded:
Bachelor
Master
Doctorate

Most Popular Majors:
18% Business, Management, Marketing
16% Engineering
13% Agriculture
11% Social Sciences
9% Biological and Biomedical Sciences

Undergraduate Schools:
College of Agriculture and Life Sciences
College of Architecture
College of Education
College of Geosciences
College of Liberal Arts
College of Science
College of Veterinary Medicine
Dwight Look College of Engineering
George Bush School of Government and Public Service
Mays Business School

Full-Time Faculty:

1,813

Faculty with Terminal Degree:

92%

Student-to-Faculty Ratio:

20:1

Average Course Load:

15 hours

Graduation Rates:

Four-Year: 32%
Five-Year: 64%
Six-Year: 76%

AP Test Score Requirements

Possible credit for scores of 3 or higher

IB Test Score Requirements

Possible credit for scores of 3 or higher

Did You Know?

For a nominal registration fee, **www.pickaprof.com** offers ratios of each professor's grade distributions, as well as comments and criticism from students who have taken their classes.

Texas A&M is getting more selective due to **the "Top 10 Percent Rule**." However, they have instituted a program with Blinn Community College, only several miles away from A&M, that allows Blinn students to transfer in more easily after a year or two. Some students think it's a great idea to go to Blinn and get your basic requirements out of the way before coming to A&M.

For good luck before tests, students leave pennies at the feet of **the statue of Sul Ross** in front of the Academic Building.

The journalism department was **recently disbanded** due to lack of faculty and budget cuts.

Sample Academic Clubs:

Aggie Master Gardeners Club, American Institute of Chemical Engineers, Business Administration Society, Society of Professional Journalists

Best Places to Study:

Browsing Library, Evans Library, Research Park

Students Speak Out On...
Academics

"Part of the A&M experience is about finding good teachers. It doesn't matter where you go, there are going to be good ones and bad ones."

Q "All my professors have been very helpful and nice. They are extremely challenging, but they also **care a lot for their students** and try to help you out as much as they can."

Q "**Every professor I've had is friendly**, helpful, and willing to do whatever it takes for you to learn."

Q "I think **our school is very academic-minded**, and most professors that I have run into are very helpful if you show you care about your work and education."

Q "All of the professors I've had since I was a freshman were really nice, understanding people. **They love to teach** and give you a good taste of the different professions that are out there."

Q "If you're in a difficult major, of course your classes and teachers may be harder, but **they've always been willing to help me** outside of class if I made the effort."

Q "I really liked most of the teachers I have had. Some of them are just there to do research and don't really care about us, but **a lot of them are really nice**. If you are a science major, you are more likely to get the ones that don't care or have bad English, but I had a teacher last semester that let me borrow her textbook before every test because I lost mine. She had my cell phone number and I had her home phone number!"

Q "**Some are good and some suck**. It all depends on your major. If you are going to do engineering, you will have to deal with a lot of foreigners who don't speak English very well. Get to know your professors, because they can be a great tool."

Q "**Teachers here are good**. Every once in a while you run across a professor you might not get along with, but that happens anywhere."

Q "Before you register, **look the professors up on *pickaprof.com***. It helps so much to hear what other people say about them. That's how I've chosen every class I've taken."

Q "You have the good and the bad teachers here. The **problem is that classes are usually very large**, and it is hard to get a hold of the teachers or to really get to know them. Everything is done by the Internet: homework, questions, everything."

Q "My very first teacher was **an international grad student with a thick accent**, and she kept saying the notes were on the *veb*. I couldn't find the veb and didn't understand until weeks later, when I asked someone and they clarified. The notes were on the Web—I had trouble in that class."

Q "A lot of my teachers have not been great at teaching because **there are so many people in the classes**. They often use Power Point presentations, but there is a lot of help you can get. Many classes have free tutors, and all the teachers I've had were very helpful. They have office hours and are willing to help you succeed. Of course, there are always a few really terrible teachers who want nothing to do with their students, but I've come across very few of them."

Q "Like anywhere else, there are professors here who are **more interested in research than teaching**, but most are pretty good and some are really excellent. I've had pretty good experiences in most of my classes."

Q "I dropped a class because the teacher was from China, and **if I closed my eyes I couldn't understand her**. I have trouble concentrating as it is!"

Q "**There are lots of cool professors**, but there are some that suck. Sometimes, they are more interested in their research than in teaching."

The College Prowler Take On...
Academics

Professors at A&M get mixed reviews. Some are good and some aren't, but most seem to accommodate the students as much as possible, which can be a difficult task with large class sizes. Most of the teachers at A&M are extremely qualified in their field and very knowledgeable in their subject matter. There are a large number of international graduate students that may teach introductory courses, and students may have trouble deciphering some of the thick accents, but if you make an effort in their classes, chances are, they will go out of their way to help you understand whatever might be confusing you.

Academically, a lot is up to the student. Students need to make the effort to get to know the professors. In really large classes, students might have to teach one another what got skimmed over in class, or they may have to ask questions (even the shy types). Although most freshman courses have several hundred students, the professors are pretty down-to-earth. The secret to any course at A&M is to visit the professors during their office hours and get to know them. Do this, and you'll instantly become their pet; you'll get better grades, and you'll learn a lot more about the teacher as a person. The teachers actually view their students as fellow human beings, and not just some pesky pupils waiting for the bell to recess.

B-

The College Prowler® Grade on
Academics: B-

A high Academics grade generally indicates that professors are knowledgeable, accessible, and genuinely interested in their students' welfare. Other determining factors include class size, how well professors communicate, and whether or not classes are engaging.

Local Atmosphere

The Lowdown On...
Local Atmosphere

Region:
South

City, State:
College Station, TX

Setting:
Rural college town

Distance from Houston:
1 hour, 15 minutes

Distance from Austin:
2 hours

Distance from San Antonio:
2 hours, 30 minutes

Distance from Dallas:
3 hours

➔

Points of Interest:

Dixie Chicken

George Bush Presidential Library

Kyle Field

Messina Hof Winery

Closest Shopping Mall or Plaza:

Post Oak Mall

Closest Movie Theaters:

Cinemark Hollywood U.S.A.
1401 Earl Rudder
Freeway South
(979) 764-9692

Major Sports Teams:

Dallas Cowboys (NFL)

Dallas Mavericks (NBA)

Dallas Stars (NHL)

Houston Astros (MLB)

Houston Comets (WNBA)

Houston Rockets (NBA)

Houston Texans (NFL)

City Web Sites

www.cstx.gov

www.bcsclubs.com

Did You Know?

Fun Facts about College Station:

- **It's a sister city to Bryan**. Bryan is the older, more historic city with interesting hole-in-the-wall restaurants and sites. College Station is becoming increasingly more suburban.
- College Station is **expanding south**.
- **The armadillo** is the official state mammal.
- There is a **no-smoking policy in all buildings** and restaurants before 10 p.m., excluding bars and clubs.
- College Station is home to **over 67,000 people**.
- There are over **1,100 acres of public parks** in the area.
- The month of December is "Christmas in the Park." Every year, **Central Park is decorated with over half a million twinkle lights**. There are free hayrides, visits with Santa, and even hot cocoa and Christmas cookies.

Famous People from College Station:

Mary Beth from MTV's *Road Rules, South Pacific*

Students Speak Out On...
Local Atmosphere

> "A&M is unique because the town it's in, College Station, is very small and nice. The University is it—the town wouldn't be there if the University wasn't."

Q "**The town completely caters to the University**. It's awesome."

Q "The College Station and Bryan areas **totally circle around A&M**."

Q "There is **a good band scene here**, with lots of talented students. There is always an awesome 'Battle of the Bands' contest, and there are also a lot of cool, popular bands that stop through College Station on their tours. I've seen the Toadies here, as well as Blue October and Vertical Horizon."

Q "The town caters to students quite a bit. There is a community college, Blinn, in Bryan, and many Aggies take classes there as well. **You'll meet a lot of people from Blinn when you go out**. The Bryan/College Station area is generally pretty safe, though there are some rougher areas in Bryan and, to a lesser degree, in C.S."

Q "The town here is **pretty small, and it's dominated by A&M**. The community is very supportive of A&M and its students, from what I have encountered."

Q "**I hate College Station**. I made a T-shirt that says 'College Station Sucks' that has been wildly popular. I'm thinking of selling it. I could make a million."

Q "We are pretty much the atmosphere—it's Aggieland. **The town is kind of made up of us**. The only other college near by is a community college, Blinn College, in Bryan."

Q "The atmosphere is that of a college town. There is a college called Blinn, where some people co-enroll to get easy stuff out of the way while taking harder courses at A&M, but that's it for other schools. There's nothing to stay away from, but **you have to visit the George Bush library** and the Dixie Chicken, a bar, if you come."

Q "I love artsy stuff and was very disappointed coming here. There are **very few cultural things to do**, with hardly any museums or exhibits in sight. The closest things to art are some tiny exhibits in the MSC that change every few months. Go to Austin or Houston if you want that kind of stuff."

Q "**The atmosphere is really good**. Coming from Dallas, a huge city, I think we're in a pretty small town. There is not really a downtown because the College is the main thing, but Bryan has a cute little downtown right next to C.S. Austin is an hour and half away, and Houston is the same. Galveston and the beach are two hours from us. We did a bunch of little weekend road trips around Texas. There are all kinds of other little bars and clubs and stuff in C.S., too. There's a community college, Blinn, where people usually go if they don't get into A&M."

Q "**You can walk up to total strangers** and start conversations with them. That's what sold me on going to A&M."

Q "**I miss Houston**. I miss my hairdresser that really knows how to cut hair. I miss having an endless amount of options for things to do on a Friday night. I'm not really cut out to live in a small town."

Q "**College Station is a wonderful town**, and everyone is really helpful and friendly."

Q "I like College Station. Sometimes it seems like **the town is so small, and there is nothing to do**. The good part about that is that you can hang out with friends and focus on cultivating deep relationships instead of focusing on what you're doing or where you're hanging out."

Q "There are not too many places to visit, but **Austin is not far, and it provides good entertainment** if you need to leave town. There are no other colleges nearby, except Blinn, a local university pretty much made up of all A&M students. It's a very friendly atmosphere, made to accommodate college students who attend A&M."

Q "**College Station is a small town**. There aren't any other universities or stuff worth seeing in the town."

The College Prowler Take On...
Local Atmosphere

College Station is a small town in rural Texas. The town definitely revolves around A&M, and for students coming from large cities, it will take some time to adjust. There's definitely stuff to do here, but it is limited. If students do get bored—and they will—they can always take a quick road trip to Austin or Houston, both of which are only a couple hours away and offer an endless supply of things to do. The cultural scene in College Station is lacking, but there does seem to be a good music scene. The entire city works around the University's calendar, especially the athletic events. When there are home football games, it seems like the whole city shuts down to drive to Kyle Field—students wear maroon polos and sport an Aggie flags on their car antennas.

Overall, the town is very conservative. If you drive down George Bush Drive, you'll pass the Barbara Bush Conference Center on your left, then the Bush School of Government and Public Service—which sits right next to the George Bush Presidential Library. College Station is also located near the Bible Belt. Overall, there is a thick conservative and Christian atmosphere in and around College Station, but it may not be the atmosphere that everyone is looking for. It's safe to say that people either love or hate College Station.

The College Prowler® Grade on
Local Atmosphere: C+

A high Local Atmosphere grade indicates that the area surrounding campus is safe and scenic. Other factors include nearby attractions, proximity to other schools, and the town's attitude toward students.

Safety & Security

The Lowdown On...
Safety & Security

Number of A&M Police Officers:
54

A&M Police Phone:
(979) 845-2345

Safety Services:
Corps Escort Service
(979) 845-6789

Health Center Office Hours:
Monday–Friday 8 a.m.–5 p.m.

Health Services

Beutal Health Center can diagnose and treat most minor ailments that students may face. If you get sick after hours, you can "Dial-a-Nurse," which means that you can call and speak to a nurse who will give you medical advice. Student Health Services also provides on-site pharmaceuticals. A Specialty Clinic and Women's Clinic are also available on campus.

Did You Know?

Beutal Health Center is more commonly referred to as **"The Quack Shack**." But hey, it is free.

Students Speak Out On...
Safety & Security

"Security on campus is really great. I stayed on campus my freshman year and felt completely safe walking around at night alone, whether going to the library or walking to an intramural game."

Q "**Security is very good**. I think we were rated the safest campus in Texas last year. It is well lit pretty much everywhere, and you can get a Corps escort if you don't feel safe walking across campus alone at night."

Q "I lost my wallet once and got it back from Lost and Found with all the money still in it. A&M really is a cool place, and **people look out for each other**."

Q "**Security and safety around campus are very good**. I'm not sure, but I think we have one of the lowest crime rates in the nation."

Q "The **campus is pretty secure**. You see University Police Department (UPD) officers around at all hours of the day."

Q "I feel completely and **totally safe at all times**! It really is a very safe campus."

Q "The **security at A&M is pretty good**. I didn't hear of any really big problems during my first year there."

Q "The **Corps escort service is awesome**. I call them all the time. That's how I met my boyfriend. I called and he came to walk me back to my dorm!"

Q "The **on-campus security is great**. If you are out late, you can always call one of the Corps guys to escort you home. There are lots of lights, and people are always out. I personally do not like to walk around alone at night, but it's never a problem at A&M."

Q **"The campus is well lit**. and security is good, but you don't really have to worry about anything happening."

Q "Security is great. **Rarely do bad things happen**—it's a very safe town."

Q "The campus is very safe, and **there are free campus phones at various locations**."

Q "**Campus is very safe** thanks to the Corps of Cadets."

Q "Security and safety are great. If you are alone at night on campus, **you can call and get an escort** to take you wherever you need to go."

Q "The security is great. I am a female, and **I don't feel unsafe walking around campus** by myself."

Q "Safety is really good on campus. I have never felt unsafe, and if you ever do, **there's a number to call for Corps escorts** on your identification card."

Q "I don't know why people say College Station is so safe. My duplex got broken into over Spring Break, and they took my jewelry and all our electronics. **This is still a city with normal criminals**. Just because people 'feel' safe, it doesn't mean the town is perfect."

Q "This campus is very safe. **There are people walking around constantly**, even late at night, and there are always security guys around—not to mention all the lights. These are the benefits of being at a big school— the campus never goes to sleep. The worst thing that happened to me was when my bike got stolen!"

Q "**I've had three bikes stolen**. I finally just bought a cheap one from Wal-mart, and I haven't had it jacked yet."

Q "I know **several girls who've been raped on campus** walking to their dorms at night. It still is not safe to walk around by yourself. Play it safe, even when you feel safe."

The College Prowler Take On...
Safety & Security

Most students feel extremely safe on campus. There is a strong sense of camaraderie, and Aggies look out for other Aggies. There are bike thefts here and there—a lot of students have expensive bikes, and there is really no way to track them. However, living inside the Aggie Bubble leads many people into believing they're always safe. In the not-so-distant past, there have been reported cases of assault, and even rape, on campus. This is not to mention the crimes on campus that are not detected, mentioned, or reported.

However, A&M does a lot to protect their students. If you're on campus, you can call the Corps of Cadets escort service at any time of the night and get a Corps member in uniform to walk you to your car. A lot of students take advantage of this service, especially at night. Safety is something every student needs to be actively conscious of. Never walk alone or put yourself into potentially dangerous situations, no matter how safe you think you might be. Texas A&M does a lot to curb crime on campus, including trying to keep the campus well lit at night. You'll hear a lot about bike theft, but that doesn't mean that it's the only crime that exists.

B

The College Prowler® Grade on

Safety & Security: B

A high grade in Safety & Security means that students generally feel safe, campus police are visible, blue-light phones and escort services are readily available, and safety precautions are not overly necessary.

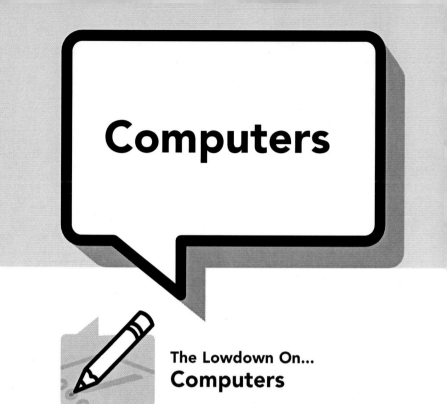

Computers

The Lowdown On...
Computers

High-Speed Network?
Yes

Wireless Network?
Yes

Number of Labs:
6

Number of Computers:
1,307

Operating Systems
Windows XP Professional

Computer Labs

Most labs contain special equipment, like LaserGraphics Personal LFR Plus, Digital Video Capture/Record Workstation, Nikon LS2000 Slide Scanner, Gateway Wireless Laptops, USB Floppy Drives (for IMACs), Compaq PentiumIII 866 (Linux Machines), Pinnacle Digital Video Capture/Edit Stations

Blocker
Located on the north side of campus across Ireland Street from the North Parking Garage, Blocker provides a 32-computer classroom, equipped with a Proxima Projector 5600, located in Room 132.

Read
Near the G. Rollie White Coliseum and the Memorial Student Center, this facility provides a 31-computer classroom. No one knows about this lab, so it's never busy.

Student Computing Center
The largest lab, open 24 hours. You can always find a computer here. It's located in the center of campus by Evans Library. There are two floors and a central help desk. Parking is difficult, but try the yellow lot by the Administration building after hours.

West Campus Library
This is by far the busiest lab and most crowded, since it is the only West Campus lab. It has a 41-computer classroom, equipped with a Proxima DPS-5640 Projector. It's also the only lab with convenient parking after hours; there's a yellow lot right behind it.

Wisenbaker
Located in Room 24 in the basement of the Wisenbaker Engineering Research Center, is the Wisenbaker computer lab, which no one knows about, so it's never crowded at all.

Discounted Software

Front Page 2002 for Windows $5

SPSS $30

Visual Studio.net Professional for Windows $20

Windows XP Professional upgrade $5

Microsoft Office XP $15

Free Software

TAMU software

Pegasus e-mail

McAffee Anti-Virus Scan

24-Hour Labs

Student Computing Center

Charge to Print?

Each student has a 150 page allotment included in their tuition, which equates to a 15 dollar limit, with each black and white page costing 10 cents and additional charges for transparencies, color, or large-format printing.

Students Speak Out On...
Computers

"There are lots of computers on campus, and everything's kept extremely updated. The school replaces the lab computers once every three semesters, so there are always new programs on the computers."

Q "There are **several computers labs on campus**. I go to the Student Computing Center (the SCC) quite often in-between classes. You get a login ID when you go to new student orientation, and you can download programs like Instant Messenger, so your information comes up regardless of what computer you log into. When you walk in the lab, it usually looks crowded, but I've always found a computer with no problem. There are two floors, and there are tons of other computing places on campus. The dorms all have super-fast Ethernet connections, too."

Q "**The computer helpdesk line is on speed dial on my phone**. If you ever have a problem with your computer, they're always sitting around waiting to help."

Q "Computer labs are readily available on campus, and **bringing your own PC is not necessary**."

Q "I got along fine without a computer because there was a lab close to my dorm. A lot of people had computers, and **I kind of wish I did, just because of the convenience**."

Q "The Ethernet gets you on the **Internet as fast as your computer can handle** it. It's so cool, and it goes so fast for downloading and file sharing."

Q "I have my own computer, and it makes everything very convenient, but if you don't have the money, or just don't want to bring one, **there is a very large student computing center**. It's usually open and doesn't get too crowded, except around finals time. I haven't really used it a whole lot, so I can't tell you much, but it is available."

Q "**The Internet runs like a breeze**. It's a great, really fast connection. I brought my computer with me, but at times I'd go to the lab. They charge computer fees whether you use them or not, so I might as well use them from time to time. The computer labs are only crowded during finals."

Q "It is always nice to have your own computer, but **the labs on campus are excellent**."

Q "Bring your own computer, for sure. **The SCC is a good place to go**, and it isn't really crowded unless we're having midterms or finals, but you'll want to bring your own."

Q "Bringing your own computer is always good, because **around finals, the labs get crowded**. The network system is good and works well in your dorm or in the lab."

Q "**You can usually find a computer to work on**, but it is more convenient to also have your own, especially if you live off campus."

Q "**The print allotment really ticks me off**. There's a really small page number [150] that they allow you to print, and after that, you have to pay. We had to do these projects for statistics that ate up my allotment, and I ended up having a pretty large fee."

Q "It is very nice to have your own computer. It saves lots of trips to computer labs, but **there are multiple labs, and you can always find a computer**."

Q "I have never really used the computer labs, but I haven't heard many complaints from those who have. The **campus network is free to students**, so it is nice to have your own computer, if it's an option."

Q "I remember **one time the power went out in the SCC**, and you heard 200 collective screams from people that hadn't saved their work. I think that was a fluke, though. I've never heard of any other problems with the system going down."

Q "**I would bring a computer or a laptop**, if I were you. It's more convenient."

Q "**A&M has a deal with Microsoft**, and you can get free and cheap software if you're a student. I know you can get Windows XP for pennies, which is highly-coveted software right now. They also have a deal with Verizon, and you can get discounted DSL service for off-campus computers."

The College Prowler Take On...
Computers

Most students agree that the computer system at A&M is more than adequate. The lab facilities are nice and big, and there are several of them around campus. You should bring your own computer, because there are very fast Ethernet connections in the dorms and working in your room is more convenient for writing last minute papers. The network is great for file sharing and downloading, and you can even access it from an off-campus computer. The only thing that can be annoying is the limit on how many pages you can print for free. One-hundred and fifty pages may seem like a lot at first, but you'd be amazed at how quickly it gets used up. If you have your own printer, it's advisable that you bring that, too. Once you use up your allotted number of free pages, it's probably more convenient to print everything in your room.

Texas A&M has deals with almost every major company in the U.S., including Coca-Cola, Nike, Verizon, and Microsoft. The good thing about these deals is that students get discounts and cool promotions. The computer deals, like discounts on various Microsoft products, are a steal and really benefit the students at a minimal cost. A&M has great labs, but knowing how to do things yourself can sometimes be less irritating. Whatever you do, just be careful not to waste all your time on Instant Messenger.

B-

The College Prowler® Grade on
Computers: B-

A high grade in Computers designates that computer labs are available, the computer network is easily accessible, and the campus' computing technology is up-to-date.

Facilities

The Lowdown On...
Facilities

Student Center:
Memorial Student Center

Athletic Center:
Recreation Center on
West Campus

Libraries:
Cushing Library
Evans Library and Annex
West Campus Library

Popular Places to Chill:
MSC Flagroom
Poor Yorick's
Research Park (West Campus)

Campus Size:
5,200 acres

What Is There to Do on Campus?

Besides classes, you can hang out in the Memorial Student Center, "the living room" of Texas A&M, where there is a bowling alley, game room, visual art gallery, and much more. You can work out at the Recreation Center or take a long walk around campus. If you just feel like sitting around, you can always grab a cup of coffee and chat with friends.

Movie Theater on Campus?

No, but there are movies shown at reduced prices sometimes.

Bowling on Campus?

Yes, in the basement of MSC

Bar on Campus?

No

Coffeehouse on Campus?

Yes, Poor Yorick's, Rumors

Favorite Things to Do

Watch people do the dance arcade machine in the basement of the MSC. There are also lots of other games and a bowling alley. Students love to hang out at Rumors, go to events held by different student organizations, or just go to parties.

Did You Know?

Don't walk on the grass around the MSC or wear your hat inside it. The Memorial Student Center is **a memorial for people who have died** in our country's wars. That may be the only time Aggies are mean—when they tell you to take off your hat or get off the grass.

The University has recently finished building **an underground walkway tunnel** for students to cross over to West Campus without being stalled by the train.

Students Speak Out On...
Facilities

"The Browsing Library is my little study secret. It is always quiet, and you can get headphones to listen to any CD they have there while you study. It's on the second floor of the MSC."

Q "The Rec is a multi-million dollar facility, housing an extremely nice weight room and workout facility, a rock-climbing wall, basketball courts, indoor volleyball courts, indoor soccer facilities, racquetball courts, aerobics rooms, an indoor running track, an indoor Olympic-sized pool, an outdoor pool, outdoor basketball courts, and sand volleyball courts."

Q "We have an enormous, three-story recreational center with a lot of equipment. There are times when it is really crowded, but you can usually get in and do what you want. The student center is nice, and there are quite a few computer labs around campus."

Q "Every student is charged a huge fee for use of the Rec Center, even if they don't use it. I wish it would be pro-rated or something. A&M really nails us with fees."

Q "We have one of the best recreational centers in the nation, with outdoor and indoor swimming pools, every kind of court you can imagine, a weight room, aerobics rooms, and more."

Q "Our workout complex, called the Rec, is huge, really new, and nice. There's a giant rock-climbing wall and a ton of stuff to do. It's three-stories high and packed with neat things on each floor."

Q "**Everything is excellent**, but our student rec center is probably the most impressive."

Q "**I like to go to the Rec** to check out the guys."

Q "I think our rec center is the biggest in the nation. **The SCC is big**, and the Student Center (Memorial Student Center) is a very popular place."

Q "**The MSC is great**—there is always something going on, and you'll always see someone you know in there."

Q "The track is on the third floor and has really good terrain. It's great to run on, because **it's always too hot outside**."

Q "Everything is awesome. It's all new or recently upgraded. **You always see something being done on campus**."

Q "**I like the hot-tub the best**, except sometimes there are really old people in it that pay for water-aerobics classes."

Q "I'm on the gymnastics team, and our facilities are okay, but it's just a club sport, so they don't really care too much about us. **The computers are good and our MSC is really nice**."

The College Prowler Take On...
Facilities

Most students are very happy with the facilities at A&M. The libraries are nice, and the Memorial Student Center is the Grand Central Station of campus. It has everything you could possibly want, from practical things, like a post office, to the entertainment of a game room and bowling alley. The Rec Center is state-of-the-art. There is a rock-climbing wall inside, as well as a nicely stocked weight room, racquetball courts, inside and outside pools, and a hot tub. There is everything here that a student could possibly want, but there are negatives that go along with that, too.

The large portion of students' tuition fees that goes into athletic facilities almost seems worth it, given the quality of the center. The libraries are so big that sometimes you can be standing around a million books and not find one that you need, but the workers are really helpful. All you need to do is ask, and they'll stick by you until your research is done and you have what you need. Overall, the facilities are great. If a facility is not new already, it's probably under construction for upgrades. A&M gives a lot of attention to making students happy and satisfied with their facilities.

The College Prowler® Grade on

Facilities: A

A high Facilities grade indicates that the campus is aesthetically pleasing and well-maintained; facilities are state-of-the-art, and libraries are exceptional. Other determining factors include the quality of both athletic and student centers and an abundance of things to do on campus.

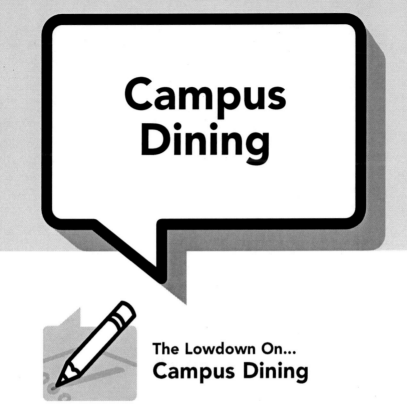

Campus Dining

The Lowdown On...
Campus Dining

Freshman Meal Plan Requirement?
No, only for Corps of Cadets

Meal Plan Average Cost:
$495.24 for five meals per week

$1445.14 for 20 meals per week

Places to Grab a Bite with Your Meal Plan:

12th Man International

Location: MSC

Food: Olla Roja Mexican, O'l Armydillos BBQ, Elephant Wok Pan Asian

Favorite Dish: Quesadillas

Hours: Monday–Friday 8:30 a.m.–2:30 p.m., Saturday–Sunday closed

→

Ag Café

Location: West Campus

Food: Chick–fil–A, Sargino's Italian, West Side Deli, al fresco salads, pizza, sandwiches

Favorite Dish: Chicken nuggets

Hours: Monday–Thursday 7:30 a.m.–4:30 p.m., Friday 7:30 a.m.–3 p.m., Saturday–Sunday closed

Commons C–Store

Location: Southside

Food: Cafeteria style

Favorite Dish: Hamburgers

Hours: Monday–Thursday 7:30 a.m.–12 a.m., Friday 7:30 a.m.–10 p.m., Saturday–Sunday closed

Duncan Dining Center

Location: Southside, Corps area

Food: Cafeteria style

Favorite Dish: Chicken fingers

Hours: Monday–Thursday Breakfast 6 a.m.–8:30 a.m., Lunch 10:15 a.m.–3 p.m., Dinner 5 p.m.–7:30 p.m., Friday Breakfast 6 a.m.– 8:30 a.m., Lunch 10:15 a.m.– 3 p.m., Saturday–Sunday closed

Hullabaloo!

Location: Basement of MSC

Food: Custom deli sandwiches, pizza, pasta, burgers

Favorite Dish: Chicken strips

Hours: Monday–Thursday 10 a.m.–8 p.m., Friday 10 a.m.–4 p.m., Saturday–Sunday closed

Rumours Coffee House & Deli

Location: MSC

Food: Deli

Favorite Dish: Chicken caesar rollup

Hours: Monday–Thursday 7 a.m.–1 a.m., Friday 7 a.m.– 12 a.m., Saturday–Sunday 8 a.m.–12 a.m.

Sbisa Dining Center

Location: Northside

Food: All-you-can-eat buffet, pizza, international, hamburgers, Chick-fil-A

Favorite Dish: Make your own waffles

Hours: Monday–Friday Brunch 7 a.m.–3 p.m. Dinner 5 p.m.–7:30 p.m., Saturday Brunch 8 a.m.– 2 p.m., Sunday Brunch 8 a.m.– 2 p.m., Dinner 5 p.m.–7:30 p.m.

Off-Campus Places to Use Your Meal Plan

Most of the restaurants in town take Aggie Bucks.

24-Hour On-Campus Eating?

Nothing but vending machines.

Student Favorites

12th Man—there's a "quiet side" and a "loud side," where lots of groups meet for lunch. It gets very boisterous.

Other Options

You could always order delivery from one of the places in town, maybe a place that will take Aggie bucks. You could also try cooking for yourself in one of the dorm kitchenettes.

Did You Know?

There are guest meals that come **free with every meal plan purchase**. For example, if you purchase a plan with five meals per week, you get five free guest meals for the semester, so your friends that don't go to A&M—or your parents—can eat free with you on five seperate occasions. Most students don't know about these, and it's a great resource if someone drops in for a visit.

Students Speak Out On...
Campus Dining

{ "Food on campus is alright. The Sbisa Dining Center, a huge cafeteria, is pretty good, as is Hullaballoo!, which is located in the MSC Underground."

Q "**The food is decent**. It gets old after a while, but there is plenty to choose from. Options depend on where you live. On Southside, there is a Chick-fil-A, a sandwich shop and a cafeteria. On Northside, there is a Chick-fil-A, a smoothie shop, a sandwich and salad place, and a cafeteria. In the center of campus, there's a coffee shop and sandwich place called Rumors, plus Hullaballoo!, which has pizza, sandwiches, chicken, and chicken fried steak."

Q "**Sbisa is like a wonderful food dream**. You walk in and it's like an acre-wide buffet serving everything you can think of. I run them out of money since it's all-you-can-eat. You can always get your money's worth from your meal plan."

Q "The food isn't horrible, but after a while, you get kind of tired of it. **We do have Chick-fil-A and Whataburger** on campus, which make up for the cafeteria food at times."

Q "The food is okay. In the Underground, an eating place on the north side of campus, there is a Whataburger, a Chick-fil-A, an ice cream place, and a salad and sandwich place. Southside there is a pizza place, which is very good, and another Chick-fil-A. There are many other **very good restaurants that all take Aggie Bucks**, which are prepaid dining dollars, or the meal plan."

Q "**The best are the breakfast tacos at the 12th Man—** they are awesome. Breakfast at most cafeterias is good, as long as you can wake up in time to eat there."

Q "No matter which dorm you choose, **you do not have far to go to find a good meal**! Both Northside and Southside dorms offer students a cafeteria including meal plans that are accepted at any on campus dining hall, cafeteria, or snack stand."

Q "The food on campus is standard for campus dining. **There are really good places around town**, but keep in mind that the whole town is geared toward college students."

Q "For a late night of studying, **Rumours is the hot spot**!"

Q "I am not too picky about food, but I can tell the difference between good and bad, and I think we have pretty good food. **I am an athlete, and we have our own dining hall**, but I have eaten at other dining halls and the food was good there."

Q "Sbisa is pretty much run by the Northside residents. They have all these traditions and yells, and **each dorm has its own personal table**. I sat at one once, and all these boys came and sat around me—it was really intimidating."

Q "I don't live on campus, but **the food that I've had has been really good** compared to the school I went to my freshman year. The dorm food isn't bad. They have a cafeteria called Sbisa with anything you can think of."

Q "I like the food a lot. **There is a ton of variety**, but I never get tired of eating Chick-fil-A. There are cafeterias on every side of campus. You never have to walk far to get something to eat."

The College Prowler Take On...
Campus Dining

Students agree that the food on campus is somewhere between average and good, and they appreciate the day-to-day variety. There are many dining facilities that offer several options, so don't worry about getting tired of any particular dish. Meal plans can be expensive, but students here do get a lot of food, and options, for the price.

There are several all-you-can eat cafeterias, giving A&M students the option of taste-testing as little, or as much, as they desire from semester to semester. There's also pizza, burgers, and everything you can think of that's both tasty and fattening. For those of you looking to fend off the Freshman 15, there are salad bars and delis where you can build your own healthy sandwiches. The best kept secret on campus is Cain Dining Hall in the athletic dorm. Athletes are catered to hand and foot, and Cain is little by little becoming known as the best cafeteria on campus, and maybe the entire city. Tuesday is steak night—and there's nothing like a good 'ol Texas-style slab of steak—but there are also other options available. Don't be afraid to try every eatery on campus when you first get to A&M. It's the only way to see what's out there and find out what you like best.

B

The College Prowler® Grade on
Campus Dining: B

Our grade on Campus Dining addresses the quality of both school-owned dining halls and independent on-campus restaurants as well as the price, availability, and variety of food.

Off-Campus Dining

The Lowdown On...
Off-Campus Dining

Restaurant Prowler:
Popular Places to Eat!

Bennigan's
Food: American grill
1505A Texas Ave. S
(979) 696-9066
Price: $8–$15
Hours: Daily 11 a.m.–1 a.m.

La Bodega
Food: Mexican
102 Church Ave.
(979) 691-8226
Price: $7–$12
Hours: Monday–Thursday
11 a.m.–10 p.m., Friday–
Saturday 11 a.m.–11 p.m.,
Sunday 8 a.m.–10 p.m.

➜

Buppy's BBQ

Food: Barbecue

506 Sulphur Springs

(979) 779-6417

Cool Features: They cater.

Price: $5–$7

Hours: Monday–Friday
11 a.m.–2 a.m.

Cheddar's Casual Cafe

Food: American grill

1701 University Dr.

(979) 260-1701

Price: $7–$15

Hours: Sunday–Thursday
11 a.m.–10 p.m., Friday–
Saturday 11 a.m.–11 p.m.

Chili's

Food: Ribs, wings, burgers

1063 Texas Ave. S

(979) 696-4261

Cool Features: Good Tex Mex

Price: $10–$15

Hours: Monday–Thursday
11 a.m.–11 p.m., Friday–
Saturday 11 a.m.–12 a.m.

Christopher's World Grill

Food: Pasta, chicken,
seafood, steak

5001 FM 158

(979) 776-2181

Cool Features: Romantic
atmosphere

Price: $10–$25

(Christopher's World Grill, continued)

Hours: Monday–Friday
11 a.m.–9 p.m. Saturday–
Sunday 11 a.m.–10 p.m.

Cotton Patch Café

Food: Home-style cooking

Highway 6 at Rock Prairie

(979) 695-9707

Cool Features: They serve
chicken fried steak with
checkered table cloths.

Price: $6–$10

Hours: Sunday–Thursday
11 a.m.–10 p.m., Friday–
Saturday 11 a.m.–10:30 p.m.

Dixie Chicken

Food: American

307 University on Northgate

(979) 846-2322

Cool Features: There are pool
tables and a patio out back.

Price: $3–$7

Hours: Daily 11 a.m.–2 a.m.

Double Dave's

Food: Pizza, pizza rolls

3505 Longmire Dr.

(979) 696-3283

Cool Features: The best pizza
rolls in town and free delivery

Price: $5–$10

Hours: Sunday–Saturday
11 a.m.–11 p.m.

Fitzwilly's

Food: American

303 University Dr.

(979) 846-8806

Cool Features: Darts, live music, TV

Price: $10–$15

Hours: Daily 11 a.m.–2 a.m.

Freebirds World Burrito

Food: The biggest burritos you've ever seen

2050 Texas Ave., 3326 Longmire Dr., 319 University Dr. and 3525 Longmire Dr.

(979) 695-0151

Cool Features: The burritos are wrapped in foil, and foil wall–art decorates the place.

Price: $5–$10

Hours: Sunday–Thursday 11 a.m.–10:30 p.m., Saturday–Sunday 11 a.m.–11 p.m.

Imperial Chinese Restaurant

Food: Chinese

2232 Texas Ave. S

(979) 764-0466

Cool Features: Buffet seven days per week

Price: $5–$10

Hours: Monday–Thursday 11 a.m.–10 p.m., Friday–Saturday 11 a.m.–11 p.m., Sunday 11:30 a.m.–10 p.m.

Jason's Deli

Food: Deli

1460 Texas Ave. S

(979) 764-2929

Cool Features: Catering, delivery

Price: $5–$10

Hours: Daily 10:30 a.m.–1 a.m.

Mi Cocina

Food: Mexican

326 George Bush Dr.

(979) 779-1411

Cool Features: For breakfast, you still get chips and salsa.

Price: $5–$7

Hours: Monday–Thursday 5:30 a.m.–10:45 p.m., Friday 5:30 a.m.–11:45 p.m., Saturday 4:30 a.m.–11:45, Sunday 4:30 a.m.–10:45 p.m.

Olive Garden

Food: Italian

2000 Texas Ave. S

(979) 696-1921

Price: $15–$20

Hours: Sunday–Thursday 11 a.m.–10 p.m., Friday–Saturday 11 a.m.–11 p.m.

On the Border

Food: Mexican

709 Texas Ave. S

(979) 695-2492

(On the Border, continued)
Hours: Monday–Thursday
11 a.m.–10 p.m., Friday–
Saturday 11 a.m.–11 p.m.

Wings 'n More
Food: Wings and more
1045 Texas Ave. S,
3230 Texas Ave. S
(979) 694-8966
Cool Features: The best wings
in town
Price: $5–$7
Hours: Daily 11 a.m.–12 a.m.

Best Pizza:
Double Dave's

Best Chinese:
Imperial Chinese Restaurant

Best Breakfast:
Mi Cocina's breakfast tacos

Best Wings:
Wings n' More

Best Healthy:
Cotton Patch

Best Place to Take Your Parents:
Christopher's World Grill

Closest Grocery Stores:
Kroger
2412 Texas Avenue South
(979) 693-9974

Albertson's
615 University Drive East
(979) 260-4200

Student Favorites:
Freebirds, Dixie Chicken,
Cheddar's

24-Hour Eating:
IHOP, Denny's, Wendy's

Did You Know?

Aggie Bucks are accepted at most restaurants off campus. **You register for them when you register for classes**, and a credit is put on your student ID card. You can then pay for meals off-campus with your ID card. Aggie Bucks are also accepted at vending machines on campus, and you are sent a monthly statement over your Neo e-mail account telling you your balance and transactions.

Students Speak Out On...
Off-Campus Dining

{ **"There are tons of restaurants in College Station. We have a lot of the major chains, as well as local places. Many of the local restaurants have a great atmosphere."**

Q "**There are great places to eat off campus**. You have to eat at Freebirds, which is one of the most popular places in town. There's one right across the street from campus. If you like buffalo wings, Wings n' More is the place to go. There are a couple of good steak houses, and also good places for Italian and Mexican food."

Q "I lived right behind **Wings n' More, and I ate there most days of the year**. They have this special sauce, which is so good you'll want to put it on everything."

Q "**Freebirds is a hot spot**, pretty famous in College Station. One of my favorites is Cheddar's, and of course, there's always the world-famous Dixie Chicken."

Q "Freebirds is an Aggie classic. It's like burritos Subway-style. **We have places like Chili's, Cheddar's**, On the Border, Olive Garden, and other chains like that, too."

Q "**Freebirds is cool**. You can go and get drinks at the bar, and the hamburgers are a couple bucks. It's a cool place to hang out over cheap food and throw darts or play shuffleboard with friends."

Q "**Freebirds is a very popular burrito place**. It's very different from most places you'll encounter down here."

Q "I love **Jason's Deli for a healthy meal**, and they give you free ice-cream, which probably 'cancels out' the healthy salad or sandwich you just had. It's good food, though, and on Mondays, they give you student discounts."

Q "We have **all kinds of restaurants off campus**, including the normal ones like Bennigan's and On the Border. We have a couple of nice streak houses. We also have some unique places like Freebirds, where they have huge burritos that no one can finish, and the Dixie Chicken, which College Station is famous for."

Q "**Christopher's is the best place to go for dates**. It's really expensive, but the atmosphere is great and really romantic."

Q "**La Bodega is the best**. It's like Mexican food, but more of a Baja grill with lots of black beans and authentic ingredients. They also have the best margaritas in the whole city."

Q "**Dixie Chicken is my favorite** spot off-campus. It's a bar with great food. Everyone knows where it is, and it's one of the most popular hangouts."

Q "College Station is a food place. Off-campus, there's a place that every Aggie has to go to called 'The Chicken,' otherwise known as the Dixie Chicken, on Northgate. **Fitzwilly's is right next door**—it definitely deserves a mention."

The College Prowler Take On...
Off-Campus Dining

For a small town, College Station offers a wide variety of restaurants. Students can find any food they crave, and there are plenty of big-name chain restaurants to choose from. College Station is home to the original Freebirds—the only restaurant in the country where an entire meal can be found in inside a single burrito. Because there's a strong international presence here, there's also a good mix of authentic international restaurants. Northgate houses many restaurants and bars within walking distance of campus. There are also some quaint little places in downtown Bryan for those special date nights.

Whether you're looking for something quick and cheap to munch on with friends or a more formal evening, there is a place for you to eat in College Station. Eating off campus is, for the most part, especially convenient because most places are close to campus and take Aggie Bucks. It's a great idea to ask your parents to put money on your ID card, so that later in the semester, when you're out of cash, you can still go out to eat with your friends. It's like a prepaid credit card.

The College Prowler® Grade on

Off-Campus Dining: A

A high Off-Campus Dining grade implies that off-campus restaurants are affordable, accessible, and worth visiting. Other factors include the variety of cuisine and the availability of alternative options (vegetarian, vegan, Kosher, etc.).

Campus Housing

The Lowdown On...
Campus Housing

Room Types:
Single suites, double suites, apartments, single rooms, double rooms

Dorm Types:
Modular, commons, balcony, corridor, and ramp dorms

Best Dorms:
Commons
Modulars

Undergrads Living on Campus:
25%

Worst Dorms:
Hart
Walton

Number of Dormitories:
27

University-Owned Apartments:
4

➡

Dormitories:

Balcony Dorms:

Balcony dorms feature single and double suite-style rooms that open onto outside balconies. Substance-free floors and housing for persons with disabilities are provided. Rooms contain built-in furniture, two ResNet connections, local telephone service (though no telephones), and basic cable TV access. Buildings provide study and TV lounges, coin-operated laundry facilities, vending machines, and resident parking.

FHK (Fowler, Hughes and Keathly complex)

Total Occupancy: 742
Floors: Four, no elevator
Rooms: 370
Coed: Yes
Location: Northside

McInnis Hall

Total Occupancy: 152
Floors: Four, no elevator
Rooms: 77
Coed: No, all male
Location: Northside

Schuhmacher Hall

Total Occupancy: 160
Floors: Four, no elevator
Rooms: 84
Coed: Yes
Location: Northside

Commons Dorms:

Commons dorms offer double suite-style rooms connected by one bathroom. Substance-free floors and housing for persons with disabilities are provided. Rooms contain ResNet connections, local telephone service (though no telephones), and basic cable TV access. Buildings provide study lounges on each floor, TV lounge coin-operated laundry facilities, snack bar, dining hall, convenience store, and mailboxes.

Aston

Total Occupancy: 470
Floors: Four, no elevator
Rooms: 235
Coed: No, all male
Location: Southside

→

Dunn

Total Occupancy: 470
Floors: Four, no elevator
Rooms: 235
Coed: No, all male
Location: Southside

Krueger

Total Occupancy: 470
Floors: Four, no elevator
Rooms: 235
Coed: No, all female
Location: Southside

Mosher

Total Occupancy: 470
Floors: Four, no elevator
Rooms: 235
Coed: No, all female
Location: Southside

Corridors:

Corridor dorms offer single suites, double suites, single rooms, and student apartments. Bathrooms are communal by floor and provide private shower areas. Substance-free floors and housing for persons with disabilities are provided. Rooms contain ResNet connections, local telephone service (though no telephones), and basic cable TV access. Buildings contain TV lounges, and Crocker Hall offers a study lounge.

Briggs Hall

Total Occupancy: 214
Floors: Four, no elevator
Rooms: 107
Coed: No, all female
Location: Southside

Crocker Hall

Total Occupancy: 246
Floors: Four, no elevator
Rooms: 123
Coed: No, all male
Location: Northside

→

Davis-Gary Hall

Total Occupancy: 246
Floors: Four, no elevator
Rooms: 123
Coed: No, all female
Location: Northside

Keist Hall

Total Occupancy: 214
Floors: Four, no elevator
Rooms: 107
Coed: No, all female
Location: Southside

Moore Hall

Total Occupancy: 246
Floors: Four, no elevator
Rooms: 123
Coed: No, all male
Location: Northside

Moses Hall

Total Occupancy: 246
Floors: Four, no elevator
Rooms: 123
Coed: No, all male
Location: Northside

Spence Hall

Total Occupancy: 214
Floors: Four, no elevator
Rooms: 107
Coed: No, all female
Location: Southside

Modular Halls:

Modular halls include private bathrooms in each room and room carpeting. Housing for persons with disabilities is provided. Rooms contain ResNet connections, local telephone service (though no telephones), and basic cable TV access. Buildings provide laundry facilities and study lounges.

Appelt Hall

Total Occupancy: 300
Floors: Four, no elevator
Rooms: 149
Coed: No, all male
Location: Southside

Clements Hall

Total Occupancy: 238
Floors: Four, no elevator
Rooms: 119
Coed: Yes
Location: Northside

Eppright Hall

Total Occupancy: 234
Floors: Four, no elevator
Rooms: 117
Coed: Yes
Location: Southside

Haas Hall
Total Occupancy: 270
Floors: Four, no elevator
Rooms: 135
Coed: No, all female
Location: Northside

Hobby Hall
Total Occupancy: 238
Floors: Four, no elevator
Rooms: 119
Coed: Yes
Location: Northside

Lechner Hall
Total Occupancy: 238
Floors: Four, no elevator
Rooms: 119
Coed: Yes
Location: Northside

McFadden Hall
Total Occupancy: 270
Floors: Four, no elevator
Rooms: 135
Coed: No, all female
Location: Northside

Neely Hall
Total Occupancy: 270
Floors: Four, no elevator
Rooms: 135
Coed: No, all female
Location: Northside

Rudder Hall
Total Occupancy: 234
Floors: Four, no elevator
Rooms: 117
Coed: No, all female
Location: Southside

Underwood Hall
Total Occupancy: 234
Floors: Four, no elevator
Rooms: 117
Coed: No, all female
Location: Southside

Wells Hall
Total Occupancy: 234
Floors: Four, no elevator
Rooms: 117
Coed: Yes
Location: Southside

→

Ramp Dorms:

Ramp dorms offer double suite-style rooms connected by one bathroom. Housing for persons with disabilities is provided. Rooms contain ResNet connections, local telephone service (though no telephones), basic cable TV access, and window air conditioning units. Buildings provide laundry facilities, a TV lounge, and study lounges.

Hart Hall

Total Occupancy: 276
Floors: Four, no elevator
Rooms: 138
Coed: Yes
Location: Southside

Walton Hall

Total Occupancy: 332
Floors: Four, no elevator
Rooms: 166
Coed: No, all male
Location: Northside

Bed Type

Generally, beds are twin and can be bunked or not bunked, but the exact mattress size varies depending on the dorm. Beds cannot be lofted off the floor in some dorms.

Available for Rent

MiniFridge with or without attached microwave

Cleaning Service?

Yes, there is a weekly cleaning service for public areas.

What You Get

Desk, bed, Ethernet connection

Also Available

University-owned apartments

Did You Know?

 In most dorms, you can bring or build a loft or a bunk bed **to leave more floor space**. Some people have lofts, and thus have room for couches.

Every Friday night, Residence Life hosts Aggie Nights in the Memorial Student Center and the surrounding area to provide **free food, entertainment, and prizes to the students** of Texas A&M University. The free entertainment includes bowling, billiards, local bands, student performing groups, game shows, comedy shows, novelty games, and more.

Students Speak Out On...
Campus Housing

"Your first decision when you come to A&M will be choosing the right dorm, but just as important is choosing between the Northside and Southside dorms."

Q "**I was really cramped in the dorms**. I had to move out because I need my space. I wanted my own room and a couch to sit on."

Q "The Commons are nice. Made up of Mosher, Kruger, Dunn, and Aston Halls, they're mostly for freshmen. I found **I really enjoyed my experience in Mosher**. The Commons is the main place on Southside. The modular dorms are really nice, too. They are pretty big and offer private bathrooms. I would suggest either the Commons or a modular dorm. Even the ones with a community bath are pretty nice, but I wanted a bathroom right there by my room. In the Commons, you and your roommate share a pretty big bathroom with two suitemates. Once a week, cleaning people clean the bathrooms in the Commons, which was really nice."

Q "**Get a modular room if you want your own bathroom**. This way, you'll only have to share with your roomie. If you want to meet people, you should get a suite at the Commons or FHK. You'll share a bathroom with three other people and have a smaller room, but the social benefits can outweigh the lower-living quality. I wouldn't recommend anywhere else, because you have to share a bath with the whole floor. I've lived in Underwood Hall, an all female dorm, and in Clements. Both are modular style, and I thought they were really nice."

Q "The **dorms can be nice**, but it depends on where you live. I don't really know which ones to avoid—except, of course, the ones without air-conditioning."

Q "Located across University Drive from Northgate, the Northside dorms are usually known to house those students who are very outward with their Aggie spirit! Though the **Southside is usually considered the quieter side of campus**, it also sits amidst the Aggie spirit that is the Fightin' Texas Aggie Corps of Cadets and their dorms. You gotta love it!"

Q "**I was in FHK and loved it**. Everyone is really friendly, and the balconies help to open everyone up to meeting their neighbors."

Q "**Don't live in Hart or Walton**. Some people like dorms on Northside, but I'd much rather stay in the dorms in Southside."

Q "The dorms were built decades ago and are older than dirt. The fluorescent lights disgust me, so we took them out and just used lamps. Depending on your roommate, you can usually dress up your room and make it feel homier. **You can bring a TV, microwave, and fridge, but there's not much room for them**."

Q "**There isn't enough on-campus housing**, so if you don't get your housing application in early, you'd better look off campus. If you end up on the wait list, you're probably better off living off campus, as well."

Q "**I would definitely suggest living on campus** your first year. I loved it, and I think it was a good experience for me. Now I love living off campus and being on my own."

Q "I'm pretty spoiled and I hate sharing things, so **I got a private room. It's a lot of money**, but I love it and the convenience of still being on campus."

The College Prowler Take On...
Campus Housing

Most dorms at A&M are pretty old, but there are many to choose from in every style and price range, from suites to singles. It's recommended that you stay on campus your first year, as it helps you meet people and feel more a part of the University. Most students do, and all seem to be very happy with that decision.

A&M is divided into two parts, Northside and Southside. Every person on each side will tell you their side is the best. The dorms on Northside are generally cheaper, and the Northside dwellers, in general, are a close-knit, anti-frat, anti-Corps group. Southside is home to the Corps Dorms and the Commons, which houses a lot of sorority girls. You'll just have to take a guess about which side you think you'd like best, because they really are very different. Some students room with friends from high school, but others prefer to go "potluck," or to just have a roommate assigned to them randomly, which is the most common way of getting a roommate. There are benefits with both, but remember it's easier to get mad at a stranger than your best friend. People always say that rooming with high school friends will ruin your friendship, and more often than not, it's true.

B-

The College Prowler® Grade on

Campus Housing: B-

A high Campus Housing grade indicates that dorms are clean, well-maintained, and spacious. Other determining factors include variety of dorms, proximity to classes, and social atmosphere.

Off-Campus Housing

The Lowdown On...
Off-Campus Housing

Undergrads in Off-Campus Housing:
75%

Average Rent For:
1BR Apt.: $525
2BR Apt.: $630

Popular Areas:
Scandia Apartments
Sterling Apartments

Best Time to Look for a Place:
Around Spring Break
(for the following year)

For Assistance Contact:
Off-Campus Aggies
http://oca.tamu.edu
(979) 845-0688
oca@stuorg.tamu.edu

"There are a lot of apartments, condos, duplexes, and houses for rent or sale. There is a free off-campus bus system now, as well, so you won't have trouble getting to and from class."

Q "I've found that **it's really convenient to live off campus**, as long as you live on the bus route. There are tons of bus routes that run all over the city, and most places are on the bus route. Apartments usually have a message indicating that they're located on the shuttle route on their fliers and ads to make sure you know. People usually look for that as a priority."

Q "Don't worry about choosing where to live right now. The summer before your freshmen year, **your mailbox will be flooded with all the options** that you can choose from."

Q "**Off-campus housing is pretty good**, for the most part. College Station is unique in that the campus is the focus of attention, so everything in town is made for the students' convenience."

Q "Don't forget there are two different towns to live in: College Station and Bryan. The electric bills in Bryan are cheaper, but **it's more ghetto**."

Q "**We rent a huge house in Bryan really cheap**. We traded space and money for the inconvenience of having to drive to school and park, but it is so worth it."

Q "**There is nothing super nice off campus**, but you won't pay more than about $400 a month, which is good."

Q "**Housing off-campus is everywhere** and is available in just about every price range."

Q "Places like **the Callaway House and Traditions are student dorm alternatives** located near campus in these massive skyscraper buildings. They are expensive, and mostly freshmen live there."

Q "**You can get much better deals off campus** than on campus. Dorms are expensive for the space you get. If you want an apartment for next year, rent now!'"

Q "**The holy grail of houses is to find one on the south side of campus**. They are cool, historical houses and so close you can ride your bike to school."

Q "The convenience of off-campus housing depends on where you live, but with **the bus system, pretty much everywhere is great**."

The College Prowler Take On...
Off-Campus Housing

Students agree that there are many options for off-campus living, just as there are with A&M's dorms. Some students prefer to live in cheaper houses in Bryan, but sacrifice the convenience of living close to campus. Living off campus can also add up, since electricity, phone, cable, and Internet bills tend to add up, but most students think it's worth it for the space alone. There are hundreds of apartments near campus, all at reasonable rates. Some say the secret is to try to get a house close to campus so you don't have to search for parking on campus. The bus system is pretty good, too. There are routes from most apartments to different spots on campus.

It's really nice having an oven and stove after living in the dorms for a year. Granted, you may not really have time to cook, but even microwave dinners seem to taste a little better off campus. You can't really host parties in the dorms, so a place off campus is a must if you want to fit more than three people on the guest list. Just make sure your housing choice gives you transportation options to campus. Since College Station really expanded around the University, some of the first things to be constructed were off-campus houses and apartments. There are new ones constantly being built as well, so you should have no problem finding a temporary home away from home.

B+

The College Prowler® Grade on
Off-Campus Housing: B+

A high grade in Off-Campus Housing indicates that apartments are of high quality, close to campus, affordable, and easy to secure.

Diversity

The Lowdown On...
Diversity

Native American:
1%

White:
82%

Asian American:
3%

International:
1%

African American:
2%

Unknown:
1%

Hispanic:
10%

Out-of-State:
3%

Political Activity

There are people from every political point of view on campus, but Republicans are definitely in the majority and are the most active on campus. This is a very conservative-minded town and school.

Gay Pride

A&M students are somewhat tolerant of the gay community. There are a couple groups for gay and lesbian Aggies, but they are definitely in the minority and are not highly visible on campus.

Most Popular Religions

Christianity is by far the most popular religion on campus. There are over 70 religious organizations on campus, from Christian fraternities and sororities, to other religious clubs like the Bahai Club, the Buddhist Student Organization, and a variety of different Muslim groups.

Economic Status

Most students here are middle-class, but of course, there are students here from every economic level.

Minority Clubs

There are about 60 minority organizations on campus—like the Asian American Association, the Hispanic Business Student Association, the African American Student Coalition, the African Students Association, the Gay, Lesbian, Bisexual and Transgendered Aggies, the Indian Students Association, and the Society for the Promotion of Indian Classical Music and Culture—but considering the immense size of campus, they are still not all that visible.

Students Speak Out On...
Diversity

"We have many different cultures, but the majority of people are white. We're a pretty conservative school compared to many others."

Q "The **campus is very diverse**, with very interesting, intelligent people."

Q "I would say we're diverse. It seems like **there are people of all races here**, but there really are a lot of white people."

Q "**A&M is like a big family**, so differences in religion or race don't really divide us much."

Q "The campus is **predominantly white**, but there is not much racial tension or conflict."

Q "You mostly see Caucasians, but there are a number of African Americans. As a Hispanic, I know we're definitely harder to find, but we're here. **A&M is very well-rounded**, I think."

Q "No, **we're not really diverse**, but the only people I hear complaining are members of the administration."

Q "**Diversity is another thing A&M doesn't have**. I'm not saying there are only white people, but the number of whites compared to the number of any other race is very lopsided. It's not a big deal, though."

Q "There are a lot of cowboys at A&M. It's not at all a diverse place. **A lot of people are the same, and most are very conservative**. There are a lot of good-looking people, but just not much diversity."

The College Prowler Take On...
Diversity

Someone coined the phrase "Caucasian Station" for this city, and the nickname is justified. A&M's campus, and the surrounding area at large, is definitely dominated by people that are white, middle-class, heterosexual, and conservative. There are people around that don't fit that description, but they just aren't nearly as visible on campus. There is not a lot of diversity, but the administration is aware of that and is taking steps to try to improve the situation. At the moment, there are many organizations on campus to raise awareness about and celebrate the diversity that does exist on campus. While these organizations may not be as strong as they could be, improvements can be made as time goes on, especially as year after year, more open-minded, diverse freshmen descend upon campus.

Most students realize the University is not very diverse, but there is little tension among students. People from almost every country and ethnicity possible can be found somewhere on campus, no matter how small their numbers may be. A&M really feels like a family, and most Aggies are generally very welcoming toward everyone, regardless of ethnicity, economic status, or sexual orientation. Still, there are always a few people less than tolerant of anyone different from themselves.

The College Prowler® Grade on

Diversity: D

A high grade in Diversity indicates that ethnic minorities and international students have a notable presence on campus and that students of different economic backgrounds, religious beliefs, and sexual preferences are well-represented.

Guys & Girls

The Lowdown On...
Guys & Girls

Men Undergrads:
50%

Women Undergrads:
50%

Birth Control Available?
Yes, the pill, the patch, and condoms are available through health services. The prices vary, depending on the specific product, but the pill ranges from $10 to $29 and condoms are 10 for $2—a very respectable price.

Most Prevalent STDs on Campus
Chlamydia

Students with an STD
12%

Social Scene

Between the southern hospitality you'll find on campus and the school pride that bonds all Aggies together, you'll find everyone on campus very welcoming. It might take you a little while to find the exact group that you fit in with best, but you won't have a hard time making friends on campus and finding people to hang out with.

Hookups or Relationships?

While you can certainly find both on campus, there are definitely more hookups than relationships. Most A&M students just want to have fun, but if you're more of a relationship-oriented person, you'll definitely be able to find someone else that also wants something more commitment-based than a one-nighter.

Dress Code

T-shirts are the chosen uniform for going to class. If you're going out at night, most people go semi-dressy—polos for guys and slacks or denim skirts for girls, but both wear flip-flops. Other than that, people wear whatever they're comfortable in.

Did You Know?

Top Places to Find Hotties:
1. Fraternity/sorority parties
2. The Quad
3. Bars/clubs

Top Places to Hook Up:
1. Harry's
2. The Hall
3. Church
4. The Rec Center
5. The Library (a bar)

Students Speak Out On...
Guys & Girls

"It's a really big campus with lots of hot guys and pretty girls. You have a large selection of guys to pick from—believe me! The trick is finding the type you are 'truly' looking for, which can be a challenge."

Q "**Texan women are beautiful**. Everyone knows that."

Q "The **Corps guys are hot**! People are nice enough, but it is hard to make friends and keep them, just because there are so many people that it's hard to stay in touch."

Q "For the most part, people are very friendly. You hear a lot about Aggies being a big family and it sounds kind of cheesy, like propaganda and stuff, but it's pretty true. We're all pretty loyal. My friends and **I frequently comment on students being attractive**—there's definitely potential here."

Q "I like the guys here that know chivalry is not dead. For the most part, **they are extremely respectful to all women**."

Q "Both **the girls and the guys are great**. It's a super-friendly campus, and we do have some major hotties here and there."

Q "I like guys in uniforms, so **all the guys in the Corps are pretty handsome** to me."

Q "We have **lots of beautiful people**. I can't really compare it to other places, because I haven't seen many other campuses, but I know we have much better looking people than my boyfriend's campus—Texas Tech."

Q "There are lots of nice looking girls. Then again, I think you will find that at many colleges. **We have a pretty good selection**—you'd like it!"

Q "There are **a lot of good-looking people in Texas**. It's known for its beautiful women."

Q "Most of the girls are hot. I know **the number of girls is greater than the number of guys**, but everyone is very nice."

Q "I think **they all look kind of the same**, which is good if you like that style. Most everyone's clean cut, and there are very few punk or skater-types."

Q "Wow, **the guys are amazing**! They're adorable, with good manners, and sweet Southern charm. Bonus points if he looks good in Wranglers."

Q "The guys are cute. **It is really conservative here**, and we get lots of cowboys, but there are people representing pretty much every type."

Q "The **guys are very nice, and there are lots of them**, too. If you like blonde guys with white complexions, we have a lot of the Texan kind of cowboys."

Q "Hell, yeah, **the guys are hot**!"

The College Prowler Take On...
Guys & Girls

Most people will notice the minute they step on campus that A&M has a collection of the prettiest people in the Southwest. Most of the guys and girls seem to be clean cut and conservative dressers, but you can find anything out of the thousands of students here.

Due to the conservative atmosphere and influence of the Corps, you will find that welcoming southern hospitality all around town and on campus. Also, most of the guys are very chivalrous. It is very common for strangers to give up their seat on the bus to a lady and to hold doors open, even if the girl is 20 feet away. In fact, people may look at a guy funny if there is a lady standing next to him on the bus and he *doesn't* give up his seat. That's just the way things are here. Selfish guys can either adapt or stay single.

The College Prowler® Grade on
Guys: A

A high grade for Guys indicates that the male population on campus is attractive, smart, friendly, and engaging, and that the school has a decent ratio of guys to girls.

The College Prowler® Grade on
Girls: A-

A high grade for Girls not only implies that the women on campus are attractive, smart, friendly, and engaging, but also that there is a fair ratio of girls to guys.

Athletics

The Lowdown On...
Athletics

Athletic Division:
NCAA Division I

Conference:
Big 12

**Males Playing
Varsity Sports:**
351 (2%)

**Females Playing
Varsity Sports:**
290 (2%)

School Mascot:
Reville VII, a border collie

Men's Varsity Sports:
Baseball
Basketball
Cross-Country
Football
Golf
Swimming & Diving
Tennis
Track & Field

→

Women's Varsity Sports:

Archery
Basketball
Cross-Country
Equestrian
Golf
Soccer
Softball
Swimming & Diving
Tennis
Track & Field
Volleyball

Intramurals:

Badminton
Basketball (3 on 3)
College Football
(Bowl challenge)
CoRec Softball
Dominoes (42 style)
Flag Football
Golf
Handball
Racquetball
Soccer (indoor)
Table Tennis
Tennis (League Play)
Track Meet
Volleyball

Club Sports:

Bowling Club
Cycling Team
Lacrosse (Men's)
Lacrosse (Women's)
Gymnastics Club
Inline Hockey Club
Fencing Club
Handball Club
Ice Hockey Team
Judo Team
Pistol Team
Polo Club
Rugby (Men's)
Rugby (Women's)
Sailing Team
Soccer (Men's)
Soccer (Women's)
Target Archers
Trap and Skeet
Ultimate Frisbee
Volleyball (Men's)
Volleyball (Women's)
Water Polo (Men's)
Water Polo (Women's)
Waterskiing
Weight Lifting

Athletic Fields

Kyle Field, Olsen Field, Anderson Track & Field Complex, Vincent-Beck Stadium, Aggie Soccer Complex, Aggie Softball Complex, Archery Room, Bright Football Complex, Freeman Arena, G. Rollie White Coliseum, Reed Arena, The University Golf Course

Getting Tickets

Order a Sports Pass when you register for classes. The Sports Pass is basically a general admissions ticket for events, although it can sometimes be hard to get. There are Web sites for people looking to rent someone else's sports pass for a game or two if they have friends coming to visit. The All Sports Passes also cost $250, which is a decent chunk of change

Most Popular Sports

Football

Overlooked Teams

Women's Soccer

Best Place to Take a Walk

Research Park

Gyms/Facilities

The Rec Center

Students Speak Out On...
Athletics

> "Football is huge down here. Our team is good, though not great, but our stadium, with a capacity of over 100,000, is always jam-packed with crazy, screaming fans."

Q "We're part of the Big 12, so when it comes to varsity sports, like football, **it's definitely a big part of what our school is all about**. I have yet to find a school with as much spirit as Texas A&M."

Q "**Varsity sports are really big here**, especially football. There are tons of intramural sports here, too, and lots of people are involved in them. Texas A&M is very proud of its unity within the student body. At football games, we have fight songs that the entire crowd knows. If you are from Texas, you have probably heard tales of the intensity of the Aggie football games! They are a blast, and I haven't missed one yet."

Q "Aggie **football is the biggest thing ever**. It's like a big party going on at the stadium. There are so many traditions that it's unbelievable. Baseball is a really big thing too, but sports are just big in general here."

Q "Varsity sports are huge! Aggies love their sports. It's a tradition. We have something called the 12th man, which basically involves standing at all sporting events for the whole game in support of our team. **There are always lots of people at the games**, which are a blast. We have yell leaders, which are hot guys that lead us in yells. It's so awesome, because everyone is in unison and it's very loud. It's tons of fun."

Q "I think **baseball games are underrated**. They are really fun, and have lots of traditions and yells. And, you also get to sit down!"

Q "**Sports are big at A&M**, especially football, and there are lots of loyal fans who keep all the traditions. All games for all sports are fun, and have lots of traditions."

Q "Football is huge, and football season is the best time of the year. A&M is rich in tradition, which makes you feel like you are part of something important. Our stadium holds around 100,000 people and sells out for all of the big games. Baseball is pretty big, too, and the games are a lot of fun to go to. The fans heckle the opposing team, and it is a lot of fun. **Intramural sports are pretty big and a lot of fun to get involved in.**"

Q "Football and baseball are the biggest sports on campus, and they're lots of fun. Everyone is always at the football games, and they show great Aggie spirit. **I definitely recommend a sports pass**, or you'll miss many of the games. It's definitely worth the money."

Q "Football is very big, with this being Texas and all. The games are so much fun! **IM sports are cool**, too, and there's a wide variety."

Q "I don't think football is as great as everyone says. It's really hot in the fall, and you have to stand the whole game until your legs feel like they'll fall off. **I'd rather watch it on TV**."

Q "**You should get a Corps date to the games**, because then you can stand on the first level and see the game better. Fish [Freshmen] have to draw tickets last, and they usually get them on the third deck—up by the clouds, birds, and the Goodyear blimp."

Q "Football is the biggest sport on campus, as far as varsity goes. **Our men and women's basketball teams aren't very good**, but they are improving. Men's baseball is a pretty big sport, and our track team also has a strong following. IM sports are pretty big, as well."

Q "Football is huge, but **nothing else is really that big** of a deal here."

The College Prowler Take On...
Athletics

Football is, by far, the biggest and most overshadowing sport at A&M. Most students enjoy football games and the traditions that go along with them. When there is a game, it seems like everyone and his mother goes. It is the place to be as a student, and the people who live in College Station, as well as alumni, also show up at the games. Baseball and women's soccer are often-overlooked sports that students enjoy, as well. Not as many people come to these games, but they are a great time, and the teams are really good.

A&M devotes a lot of money and energy to developing a nationally-ranked team, and it shows. Kyle Field is always filled to capacity with screaming fans, but this obsession with football can be quite annoying. For instance, campus employees tow everyone's car out of campus parking lots to make room for alumni and other people that are driving into town for the weekend. Athletics at a nationally-recognized university is important, but many students admit that the majority of athletic funding could be better used in other places. Realistically, there are things more important than football, but it's still really fun to go to the games and cheer your team on, especially when they're good.

The College Prowler® Grade on

Athletics: A

A high grade in Athletics indicates that students have school spirit, that sports programs are respected, that games are well-attended, and that intramurals are a prominent part of student life.

Nightlife

The Lowdown On...
Nightlife

Club and Bar Prowler: Popular Nightlife Spots!

Club and Bar Crawler:

The clubs in town offer a wide variety of places to go out. Nightlife here does tend to seem kind of cowboy-oriented, but A&M students are predominantly the people out at the clubs and bars at night, and there is always something going on.

Big Pauly's

317 University Dr.

(979) 846-2469

A bar and music venue, Big Pauly's features weekly musical events, both live music and DJs. The place may seem small and somewhat cramped during bigger shows, but this just adds to the personal atmosphere. Cover charge varies depending upon the size of event, so check beforehand.

→

Dixie Chicken

307 University Dr.

(979) 846-2322

Located on Northgate, Dixie Chicken is a popular bar and restaurant. Burgers are cheap and the beer is always on tap. There are pool tables and a good atmosphere. Baseball and cowboy hats welcome.

Fox & Hound

505 University Dr.

(979) 846-0211

This place has a restaurant, bar, pool tables, and several big screen TVs. They also serve great wings and frozen drinks. Many people dress up to go here.

Hurricane Harry's

313 College Ave.

(979) 846-1724

Harry's is right next to campus, down the street from Northgate. It's a country western bar with nightly drink specials and dancing. The most popular night is Thursdays. Located in the IHOP parking lot, a lot of people go there to eat after Harry's closes to sober up and wrap up the evening.

Salty Dog

4353 Welborn Rd.

(979) 268-4353

Salty Dog is one of the popular non-Northgate bars, located on Welborn and University, Eastgate. Just a normal bar, they have good drink specials, usually dollar wells and dollar jello shots. There's an upstairs place to sit and chill, and the bar downstairs is cool, as well. Dress is casual.

The Tap

815 Harvey Rd.

(979) 696-5570

A popular sorority/fraternity hangout, the Tap is a sports bar with nightly drink specials and live entertainment on occasion. The Tap has hundreds of beers on tap and a nice patio to hang out if it gets too loud inside. Baseball hats welcome.

The Texas Hall of Fame

649 N. Harvey Mitchell Parkway

(979) 822-2222

A music venue, bar, and dance hall, the Texas Hall of Fame (or 'The Hall' for short) is an especially popular Thursday night destination; bar drinks are 75 cents, and pitchers are $2.50 until 11 p.m. The Hall features three bars, pool tables, foozball, and darts.

Student Favorites:

Dixie Chicken

Fox & Hound

Hurricane Harry's

The Tap

Useful Resources for Nightlife:

www.bcsclubs.com

Bars Close At:

1 a.m.

Primary Areas with Nightlife:

Northgate

Cheapest Place to Get a Drink:

Lots of places have drink specials certain nights. Harry's and Salty Dog are both exceptionally cheap.

Favorite Drinking Games:

Beer Pong

Card Games (A$$hole)

What to Do if You're Not 21

Underage students can study, play pool, go to the park, participate in ice blocking, attend athletic events, go to Hurricane Harry's, hang at Sweet Eugene's coffee shop, go to concerts at Wolf Pen Creek Amphitheater, chill at Lake Bryan, go mountain biking, go to the movies, check out an art galleries, take Aggie Wrangler lessons (country-western dance), drive or walk through Santa's Wonderland, knock down some pins at Wolf Pen Bowling Center, go mini-golfing, or, if you have absolutely nothing to do, try cow-tipping.

House Parties

House parties are pretty popular for people who live in apartments around campus. Underage students are much more likely to get busted for going to the bars, then for attending a house party. House parties are generally the place to be if you're underage, but you also have to know the right people to find out about the party in the first place.

Frats

See the Greek section!

Students Speak Out On...
Nightlife

> "Given that this is a cowboy town, most of the dance places are country western, which gets frightfully boring."

Q "**The bars are pretty good**, if you like the cowboy scene. I'm not into the cowboy thing, but I still like the bars. The clubs change a lot. They shut down and re-open frequently. The Salty Dog is good, as is the Tap. If you like to drink, and you're of age, the best place to go is Salty Dog."

Q "Northgate is really fun, because if you get bored with a bar, you can go next door. **There's a lot of variety within a short walking distance**, and you can park in a nearby parking garage for only a few dollars."

Q "Bars and clubs are fun and have a big country atmosphere, but there is still a little of everything. Lots of **live musicians come here** because of all the college students. Northgate is a cool place, as are Hurricane Harry's and the Texas Hall of Fame."

Q "Most of **the clubs are country**, like the Texas Hall of Fame, otherwise known as the Hall, and Hurricane Harry's. There are some other clubs in Bryan."

Q "**All the places in Northgate have cheap food**, which is great if you would rather spend money on drinks."

Q "College Station has a strip of bars right off of campus. I don't drink, so it's not really my scene, but the hot spots are the Dixie Chicken and the Tap. There are the clubs like Hurricane Harry's with **lots of country line dancing**, booty dancing, and live music."

Q "**Northgate always has live music**, and it's cool to just hang with your friends there in a chill atmosphere."

Q "**The bars and clubs here are pretty cool**. At first, it sucked because there's a lot of country music and dancing, but you get used to it, and begin to enjoy it after a while. If you don't, we have regular clubs and bars that play other kinds of music."

Q "There are quite a few bars, and Northgate is a strip of bars within walking distance of campus. There are a few dance halls with a decent mix of country and dance music, and a few clubs, as well. It's not a big city with a lot of options, but **the clubs stay pretty crowded** and people are generally friendly."

Q "We've got a strip called Northgate with a lot of the clubs, bars and restaurants within a couple blocks of each other. Depending on what you like, we've got country music places, and some that switch between the country and hip hop, like **the Hall and the infamous Hurricane Harry's**. We've got tons of bars, like the Tap, Fox and Hound, Dixie Chicken, and there are pool halls, like Slick Willie's. We even have a comedy club, the Loose Moose. It just depends on what you like."

Q "The bars and clubs are good, but it just depends on what you like. **The biggest night of the week is Thursday**. The Tap is probably the most popular place to go on Thursday because of the drink specials."

Q "**Dixie Chicken is a popular bar**. I don't party all the time, but Hurricane Harry's is a good place; it's also very popular."

Q "I just turned 20, but **if you're lucky, you might be able to get a couple of drinks here and there**. The Chicken, Fitzwilly's, Big Pauly's, and the Hole are all good places to try."

Q "**You will get busted for an MIP** [minor in possession] if you go out and try to drink underage. There are cops everywhere on Northgate, and most of them are undercover at the bars just waiting to nail you."

Q "Off-campus, College Station is like a medium-sized town. It's got a club called the Texas Hall of Fame, which everyone calls the Hall. It's like a huge dance hall, bar, and club combined. It's really big, and they alternate between sets of country and rap songs. The transition is good, and you'll see people of all kinds there that like all kinds of music. Northgate, right across from campus, is a string of several bars and clubs. **You can park and just walk the strip, going in and out of places**. Northgate is a blast. Austin is about an hour and a half away, so we've taken a couple of road trips down there. It's such a blast to go to 6th Street. They have tons of clubs and bars there."

Q "**Texas A&M lacks any hot spots**—just think of a ton of cowboys and small-town Texas people."

The College Prowler Take On...
Nightlife

Northgate, located just across University on the north side of campus, is the most popular hangout for Aggies, with a plethora of bars and restaurants available on the block. Do yourself a favor: don't schedule an 8 a.m. class on Friday mornings, because, at A&M, the weekend starts on Thursday nights.

Besides Northgate, there are some popular country western places like Harry's and the Hall, but there are not many other types of clubs. You need to learn to two-step if you come here. This is the Deep South, and entertainment in College Station often involves country western dancing. While people are always out drinking and having fun, you might get bored if you keep going to the same handful of places you'll find in town. Once you've been here a while, you might like to broaden your horizons and check out the nightlife in Houston or Austin. They aren't too far away, and they offer a world of possibilities outside College Station. No matter how long you've been here, there's always something new and fun to do, and there's plenty of debauchery to participate in.

The College Prowler® Grade on
Nightlife: B

A high grade in Nightlife indicates that there are many bars and clubs in the area that are easily accessible and affordable. Other determining factors include the number of options for the under-21 crowd and the prevalence of house parties.

Greek Life

The Lowdown On...
Greek Life

Number of Fraternities:
31

Number of Sororities:
22

Undergrad Men in Fraternities:
7%

Undergrad Women in Sororities:
12%

Fraternities on Campus:
Alpha Gamma Rho
Alpha Tau Omega
Beta Theta Pi
Chi Phi
Delta Chi
Delta Sigma Phi
Delta Tau Delta

(Fraternities, continued)
FarmHouse
Kappa Alpha Order
Kappa Sigma
Lambda Chi Alpha
Phi Delta Theta
Phi Gamma Delta
Phi Kappa Theta
Pi Kappa Phi
Sigma Alpha Epsilon
Sigma Alpha Mu
Sigma Chi
Sigma Nu
Sigma Phi Epsilon

Sororities on Campus:
Alpha Chi Omega
Alpha Delta Pi
Chi Omega
Delta Delta Delta
Delta Gamma
Delta Zeta
Gamma Phi Beta
Kappa Alpha Theta
Kappa Delta
Kappa Kappa Gamma
Pi Beta Phi
Zeta Tau Alpha

Multicultural Colonies:
Beta Xi Chi
Beta Tau Omega
Chi Upsilon Sigma
Chi Psi Beta
Delta Epsilon Psi
Delta Kappa Delta
Delta Xi Nu
Kappa Delta Chi
Lambda Theta Alpha
Lambda Theta Phi
Omega Delta Phi
Rho Delta Chi
Sigma Lambda Beta
Sigma Lambda Gamma

Other Greek Organizations:
Greek Council
Greek Peer Advisors
Interfraternity Council
Order of Omega
Panhellenic Council

Did You Know?

There are **more members** of sororities and fraternities than there are people in the Corps of Cadets.

Students Speak Out On...
Greek Life

"The Greek organizations love to party, but also take great pride in academics. There are required study hours, and everyone pushes to get higher GPA averages than the other Greek organizations."

Q "**My roommate was Greek, and she was so cool**. She broke every stereotype I had about sorority girls. She made me want to rush my sophomore year."

Q "I was in a sorority and I loved it, but **sororities don't dominate the social scene**. There are plenty of sororities and fraternities to pick from on campus."

Q "You have to choose between going regular Greek or going multicultural Greek. They are the same in that they like to party, but there are obviously different ways of getting in. You'll definitely see **a good majority of T-shirts on campus with Greek letters on them**. I'm Greek, but Greek life is not a big deal at all."

Q "**Joining a sorority was the best way for me to meet people** and have stuff to do on the weekends. It really made me feel at home and gave me friends to run around with."

Q "**Greek life is present**, and there are lots of people involved, but it definitely does not dominate here. The Corps of Cadets is really big for guys, but isn't Greek. Lots of people get involved in Fish Camp or T-Camp as counselors. There are also lots of student government organizations—the list goes on and on. We have a large Greek organization, but it definitely is not the most dominant thing on campus."

Q "Greek life is definitely thriving and a big thing, but **I don't think it dominates the social scene**. I think the Aggie Spirit unites everyone, whereas at a lot of schools, it is the Greeks versus the non-Greeks. If you rush and pledge a sorority, you will become very involved in it, and a lot of friends you socialize with will be a part of it, but not all the time."

Q "Greek life does not dominate the social scene here. We have lots of sororities and frats, but **frat boys actually kind of get looked down upon here**. Sororities aren't looked down upon so much. I have lots of friends in them, and they love it! There are a few Christian sororities, as well. There are so many other things to join here besides Greek life."

Q "**Sororities and fraternities don't play a big part in the social scene**, so even if you don't join a sorority, there are numerous ways to meet new people and make new friends."

Q "There is a Greek system if you want it, but it's definitely not dominant. **You can do anything you want**, and there are tons of organizations to join."

Q "**Going Greek is fun**, but you don't have to be a member in any society to be popular. It's not exclusive or cliquish at all."

Q "I'm not in anything, but I still don't think it is dominating at all. I think **there are more girls involved in Greek life** than guys."

Q "**Going Greek isn't the only way to meet people**. There are hundreds of organizations and clubs to get involved in, from the skydiving team to the sailing team. Go to the MSC Open House the first week of school and look into other organizations."

Q "Greek life is **a big part of the A&M campus**. I think the sororities have about 275 members in the biggest eight of them, and the main frats have between 80 and 100 members. I was in a frat and had the time of my life making lifelong friends."

Q "Greek life is present here, but it doesn't dominate. I'm not much on Greek life, so **it's a plus for me**."

Q "There is definitely a Greek scene, but it hardly dominates. There are **many students who aren't really fond of the Greeks**, but it's there if you are interested."

Q "I'm not a big fan of the Greek life, but **I have met some cool sorority girls and frat guys**. It doesn't dominate the social scene, and everyone at A&M is very nice."

The College Prowler Take On...
Greek Life

Greek life definitely doesn't dominate the social scene, but it is very active and visible on campus. There are dozens of Greek organizations on campus, giving interested students lots of options. Greek life is good if you want to join a group to meet people and have something to do, but this can also be accomplished by joining certain clubs or organizations, as well.

Greek organizations do offer a pretty good deal, with the abundant crush parties and mixers every weekend full of beautiful people. In the past, sororities and fraternities have been small and looked down upon, but they are becoming increasingly more accepted by the general student body. If you are interested in joining a Greek organization, just make sure that you understand all that goes along with it—the dues, the time commitment, the occasional stereotype. Here's some advice: check them all out and get to know the people in the organization before you make any kind of long-term commitment. Also, don't feel any pressure to join a frat or sorority. Students who are not involved in the Greek scene can still have active social lives.

The College Prowler® Grade on
Greek Life: B

A high grade in Greek Life indicates that sororities and fraternities are not only present, but also active on campus. Other determining factors include the variety of houses available and the respect the Greek community receives from the rest of the campus.

Drug Scene

The Lowdown On...
Drug Scene

Most Prevalent Drugs on Campus:
Alcohol

Marijuana

Liquor-Related Referrals:
101

Liquor-Related Arrests:
5

Drug-Related Referrals:
15

Drug-Related Arrests:
15

Drug Counseling Programs:
The Student Counseling Center, located on the Northside, provides counseling to students. For more information, call (979) 845-4427.

{ **"I don't know much about it, except that there's some pot smoking and a little coke here and there, but nothing's too big as far as I know."**

Q "I'm sure there is a drug scene here. If you want it, I'm sure you can find it. If you're not into it, it's hard to see it. I think, for the most part, **A&M parties are known for having large quantities of alcohol**."

Q "Our **drug of choice is alcohol**."

Q "**The drug scene is almost non-existent**. People just don't do that here."

Q "There is **no drug scene at all**. Even marijuana and pills are highly uncommon."

Q "There's no big drug scene. I don't know for sure, but I've never seen it. **Occasionally there's weed**, but nothing really huge."

Q "**I haven't seen any drugs since I've been here**, and I used to see them in high school all the time."

Q "Drugs are out there, like anywhere, but they're not a huge problem. **The majority of students aren't involved**."

Q "**Austin is the place the drugs are**. College Station isn't big in that scene."

Q "**There is not much of a drug scene here**, so you should have nothing to worry about. Drinking, on the other hand, is big—very big."

Q "I know for a fact that **there are people on campus who smoke up**, but there are very few. The drug scene here is almost nonexistent. It's better that way, in my opinion."

The College Prowler Take On...
Drug Scene

There is essentially no drug scene at A&M. Most students agree the presence of drugs on campus and in the city is very unobtrusive, and the most frequently abused substance is alcohol. Alcohol is probably the only substance that all students have a wide exposure to, although other drugs are likely still available on campus. They are just harder to come by and less popular, and many students will never even see them during their four years here. Of all the illegal drugs on campus, marijuana is the most popular, but even that isn't very common.

College Station is a small town with little influence from the drug culture. It's mostly a clean town, which gives you a better chance to stay in school and pass your classes. Just make sure that you don't get caught up in the drinking and partying scene, because that can take its toll, as well. Even though you'll have the opportunity to go out and party every night, you shouldn't. After all, this is college and you're here to learn, right?

The College Prowler® Grade on

Drug Scene: A-

A high grade in the Drug Scene indicates that drugs are not a noticeable part of campus life; drug use is not visible, and no pressure to use them seems to exist.

Campus Strictness

The Lowdown On...
Campus Strictness

What Are You Most Likely to Get Caught Doing on Campus?
- Parking in the wrong place
- Underage drinking
- Doing drugs
- Vandalism

Students Speak Out On...
Campus Strictness

> "When I first started at A&M, anyone could get away with drinking. Now it's different. They are pretty strict about drugs, but there really isn't that much drug traffic at A&M anyway."

Q "**The police are strict if you get caught**. On drinking, the dorm policy is you can't have drinks unless both roommates are of age. I've known people who got caught one too many times on campus, and were kicked out. I don't know too much about drugs, but I'm sure it's the same thing."

Q "The RAs don't come and raid your room for alcohol. Unless you're obvious about it, **you can't get in too much trouble**."

Q "I think they're pretty strict if you get caught with alcohol. I went to several dorm parties my freshman year that never got busted or anything, so I think a lot of it depends on how cool the RA is and if he or she decides to really come down and bust you for it. It seems like **they are stricter about candles in the dorms than alcohol**. I saw lots of drunk people coming home late on the weekends, unbothered, but my RA came in when I had candles lit and put them out."

Q "We got people to buy us liquor every week, and we'd walk down the hall going 'clink, clink, clink,' but we never got caught. **I got in a lot more trouble with parking tickets and stuff**."

Q "**Campus police are pretty strict**, but if you really try not to get caught, you won't."

Q "You are not allowed to drink at University events. I think **some dorms are even becoming dry**, although I'm not really familiar with dorm policies. Drugs are, of course, illegal anywhere."

The College Prowler Take On...
Campus Strictness

Campus police will usually invest much of their time enforcing parking violations, rather than underage drinking. If you park illegally, they will fall from the sky like ninjas, and you will be written up immediately, but campus police doesn't really seem to care about anything else on campus. It's the RAs that enforce drinking rules, and most of them are students, too, so they don't take a terribly strict stance toward drinking. But, make no mistake, many unfortunate students are caught drinking underage on campus. It probably won't happen to you, but don't rule out the possibility.

If you're 21, it's okay to have alcohol in your dorm room. Most students on campus aren't 21, though, and should exercise caution. Don't push the limits, and you'll be less likely to have the whistle blown on you. If you're caught, there are consequences. Campus doesn't hunt you down to find out what you're doing, but if they should discover that you're doing something wrong, they are going to do something about it that you probably won't like. Other than drinking, drugs, and parking, campus police really don't worry about much.

B

The College Prowler® Grade on

Campus Strictness: B

A high Campus Strictness grade implies an overall lenient atmosphere; police and RAs are fairly tolerant, and the administration's rules are flexible.

Parking

The Lowdown On...
Parking

Approximate Parking Permit Cost:
$133

A&M Parking Services:
(979) 862-PARK
parking@tamu.edu
http://www.transport.tamu.edu

Student Parking Lot?
Yes

Freshmen Allowed to Park?
Yes

Common Parking Tickets:
Expired Meter: $25
No Parking Zone: $50
Handicapped Zone: automatic tow
Fire Lane: $50

Parking Permits

Permits can be a little expensive, and garage spots are hard to land. Your permit will only be good for a certain kind of lot, and you'll have to park there.

Did You Know?

Best Places to Find a Parking Spot
West campus (Take the bus in)

Good Luck Getting a Parking Spot Here!
Zachary lot, main campus

Students Speak Out On...
Parking

> "Parking sucks! I would highly suggest getting a garage spot, if at all possible, because regular on-campus parking is a freakin' nightmare."

Q "**Pay the extra money and get a garage spot**. Get on the waiting list as soon as possible."

Q "Parking on campus really sucks. **It's quite possibly the downfall of A&M**. You quickly learn the ways around it, though. If you live on campus and get a spot in the parking garage, you are good to go. You'll have your own spot all the time. If you have a parking lot sticker, you will have to hunt for a place. They've actually built more parking lots this year, and I've heard that it's much better now than it was when I lived on campus a year ago. If you are an off-campus commuter, you will buy a blue lot pass and you can park there. It's not too hard to find a spot, but it's just a bit of a walk sometimes. You learn to leave an extra 10 minutes for the walking time."

Q "The parking on campus is terrible. You almost have to ride the bus to school. If not, **you can park in paid parking, which is a dollar an hour**."

Q "I paid for a parking pass, but **sometimes still can't find a spot**. So, I go and pay by the hour in the Koldus garage just so I can get to class on time."

Q "To put it simply, **parking is hell**! They are doing construction, so if you don't have to bring a car, don't."

Q "Parking is terrible. If you ask an Aggie what his biggest complaint about A&M is, he or she would probably say parking—it's awful. **If you're living on campus, your best bet is to get a garage spot**. That way you have a spot with your name on it and you don't have to mess with finding a place. Otherwise, you have to search. I didn't have a garage spot my freshman year, and I never left campus because I would lose my spot when I left. There is always a spot somewhere, so it's just a matter of where. You may end up walking a long way."

Q "**Parking is probably the only thing that I hate** about Texas A&M."

Q "Let's just say that, if you live on campus, your best bet is to **try to sign up for a parking garage** as soon as possible. You might not get it until sophomore year, but it's the best you can do. First year parking is a little crazy because you always have to fight to get a spot close to the dorms."

Q "**The officers will always get you** for going one minute over your 30-minute parking spot. You can try to appeal some tickets, but you better have a good excuse."

Q "Parking sucks and always will. You can always find a spot on West Campus, though, and catch a bus to wherever you need to be on campus. **We have a really good bus system that you should make use of**, especially since you pay for it in your fees."

Q "Parking is sometimes a problem, although **they are working on new parking garages now**. You will most likely have to park a ways out and walk or ride the bus in. You pretty much have to plan on getting there early to get a parking spot if you're living off campus."

Q "**Parking is like a game** you have to learn in college. I had a car, and sometimes it was a hassle to find a spot. I had to park farther from campus than I would have liked, but overall, it's quite alright."

Q "I live on campus; if you finally get a spot in the red lot, never move your car. If we're going out, **I'll make someone else drive just so I don't lose my prime spot!**"

Q "I can always find a parking place, but **I just can't park close to main campus**, where most of my classes are. You have to take a bus, walk, or ride your bike. It's kind of a hassle, but I hear that our parking is much better than many other major schools. Dorm parking stinks."

Q "**It is only easy to park if you're a business student**, but there is a really good bus system that is easy to follow and very reliable."

The College Prowler Take On...
Parking

Commuter students seem to face the biggest difficulties when it comes to parking. The best case scenario is that you'll live on campus and snag a permanent garage spot. That way, your car is easily accessible, and you will never have to search for a spot. Whatever you do, don't think that you can park illegally, even for just a minute, and get away with it. You will always get caught parking where you're not supposed to, and the fines can add up very quickly. Also remember that unpaid fines go on your fee statement, and they can track you down anywhere on Earth.

Any campus with 50,000 students is going to run into parking problems. However, A&M, at times, seems like it has it the worst out of all universities. The campus is extremely old, and has, as a result, run into campus layout problems. A new garage on West Campus was recently completed, and new lots are being built. The teachers have the prime parking, and the students just have to fight for what's left. You're probably better off not bringing a car at all; if you do, it's best to keep it off campus.

The College Prowler® Grade on

Parking: C-

A high grade in this section indicates that parking is both available and affordable, and that parking enforcement isn't overly severe.

Transportation

The Lowdown On...
Transportation

Ways to Get Around Town:

On Campus
A&M Buses; For a bus schedule, go to *http://www.transport.tamu.edu* or call (979) 847-RIDE.

Public Transportation
Brazos Transit District (979) 779-4481

Taxi Cabs
Aa-Aggieland Cab Company: (979) 846-2285

Car Rentals
Avis, local: (979) 846-9007; national: (800) 831-2847, *www.avis.com*

Budget, local: (979) 268-0908; national: (800) 527-0700, *www.budget.com*

Enterprise, local: (979) 823-2967; national: (800) 736-8222, *www.enterprise.com*

Rent-A-Wreck, local: (979) 696-0296; national: (800) 944-7501, *www.rentawreck.com*

Sears Car and Truck Rentals, local: (979) 268-0909

➜

Best Ways to Get Around Town

Drive

Walk

A&M buses

Ways to Get Out of Town:

Airlines Serving College Station

American Airlines
(800) 433-7300
www.americanairlines.com

Continental Airlines
(800) 523-3273
www.continental.com

Airport

Easterwood Airport
1 McKenzie Terminal Blvd.
College Station, TX 77845
(979) 845-8511

How to Get There

Greyhound
(979) 779-8071

Brazos Transit District
Interurban Trolley
(979) 779-7443

Travel Agents

A&M Travel Services Inc.
700 University Drive East #102
College Station, TX
(979) 864-8881

Aggieworld Adventures
2551 Texas Avenue South #J
College Station, TX
(979) 969-5000

Students Speak Out On...
Transportation

> "You never have to wait long for the buses. There are a lot of them on each route, and they are very quick."

Q "The **campus provides bus transportation on and off campus**, so if you don't bring a car, you can still get around town. It's paid for with your student fees."

Q "**You can get to the mall from campus** via the buses."

Q "**Public transportation isn't bad**. There are A&M shuttles that go on and off campus."

Q "They **best way to get around the city is to drive**. The town is too small to have any public buses or many taxis."

Q "I hardly ever drive to class because I take the bus. The bus is the best thing ever. I practically took the bus every day. **It's not a hassle at all**. I walked outside my apartment complex, and after a 10-minute ride, it drops me off in the heart of campus. It's great."

Q "**The University has buses that will pick you up** from your house and take you to your classes. They run pretty much everyday."

Q "This isn't like towns in the Northeast. **Texas doesn't really have much public transportation**. The A&M buses are the best bet, and they're free because you pay for them with your student fees."

The College Prowler Take On...
Transportation

Because of its size, College Station doesn't have much public transportation, and the A&M bus system is the best way to get to campus and back. It has many routes throughout Bryan and College Station, including one that goes directly to the malls. It will take you pretty much anywhere you need to go, and the fee for riding the bus is included in tuition.

Public transportation at A&M is almost entirely unnecessary. The city has no real need for many taxis or buses, although they certainly do exist. It's nice if you are able to bring a car so that you can use it for grocery shopping, going out, and other leisure activities, but many off-campus tasks can be accomplished by bumming a ride off a friend or taking the A&M bus. Plus, if you can avoid having a car, you won't have to deal with paying for a permit and trying to find somewhere to park. No matter what, you will certainly not miss public transportation. It might be a little inconvenient at times, but you can live without it. The town is so small and the people are so nice that you'll be able to figure out how to get where you need to be without too much hassle.

The College Prowler® Grade on
Transportation: C+

A high grade for Transportation indicates that campus buses, public buses, cabs, and rental cars are readily-available and affordable. Other determining factors include proximity to an airport and the necessity of transportation.

Weather

The Lowdown On...
Weather

Average Temperature:

Fall: 82 °F
Winter: 59 °F
Spring: 71 °F
Summer: 94 °F

Average Precipitation:

Fall: 4 in.
Winter: 3 in.
Spring: 3 in.
Summer: 2 in.

Students Speak Out On...
Weather

{ **"The weather is hot and humid, which is great if you don't like the cold, because it really doesn't get chilly at all. In the summer and up until about October, it is very, very hot."**

Q "**Get ready to sweat** a lot."

Q "The weather is usually nice. Texas **summers are really hot, and there's not much snow in the winters**, though sometimes we get a few inches or so. We have nice springs and falls. One note: always have an umbrella in your backpack. You do enough walking on campus that if it even sprinkles and you get caught without one, you'll be soaked! We have lots of light showers in the spring."

Q "**In the spring, the weather is always great** for flying kites and having picnics."

Q "**The weather is pretty hot and unpredictable**. College Station has typical Texas weather. It can be rainy one minute and absolutely beautiful the next. It's pretty much hot year-round, though. It gets cold for a couple of months in winter, but it doesn't last too long."

Q "It's hard to describe the weather here. It's nice, but **it does get hot during the summer**. It isn't unbearable at all, though."

Q "**It changes all the time, so you never know**. It may start out being hot, then a cold front will blow in and you'll freeze to death."

Q "The weather is all right. **It gets cold in the winter**, even down into the 30s. It all depends, because Texas has weird weather. When spring comes around, it gets into the 90s."

Q "**We get a lot of rain**, so always carry an umbrella just in case. It might be sunny and pretty, and then out of nowhere there'll be rain. You get used to it, though."

Q "**Always carry an umbrella in your car**. You'll get caught at the worst times and have to go to class soaking wet."

Q "**The weather is hot and humid**, and it rains a lot in the fall. It's not the best, but in the spring, it is really sunshiny and beautiful a lot of the time."

Q "It is very hot in the summer—around 100 degrees. The **humidity is high all year**. There's not much of a winter, and the temperature rarely drops below freezing. We get good rain in the spring and fall."

Q "**It's so hot in the fall** when you're standing in the sun during football games."

Q "It's really hot in the summer, **warm to cool in the fall, cool to cold in winter**, and beautiful in spring."

Q "The weather is really nice most of the time, though it can be humid. **It doesn't ever get really cold**, but it does tend to stay hot."

The College Prowler Take On...
Weather

Texas is hot. College Station is generally hot from March to October, and it rains frequently. This combination can lead to high humidity, although College Station isn't nearly as muggy as Houston can be. Most of the time, students seem to like the weather and find it hot, but tolerable. The humidity is usually only really bad in the summer, and luckily for most college students, they're not here to experience it.

In the spring and fall, the weather is milder. It's still warm and sunny, but not unbearably so. It's great for playing sports outside, and you can wear shorts and flip flops for a lot longer than in other parts of the country. The winter here can get a little cold, but it's really nothing too severe. In general, the weather is comfortable and warm, but you should be prepared for anything, especially rain. The weather can be unpredictable at times, and no one wants to get caught walking across campus in the pouring rain.

B-

The College Prowler® Grade on

Weather: B-

A high Weather grade designates that temperatures are mild and rarely reach extremes, that the campus tends to be sunny rather than rainy, and that weather is fairly consistent rather than unpredictable.

Report Card Summary

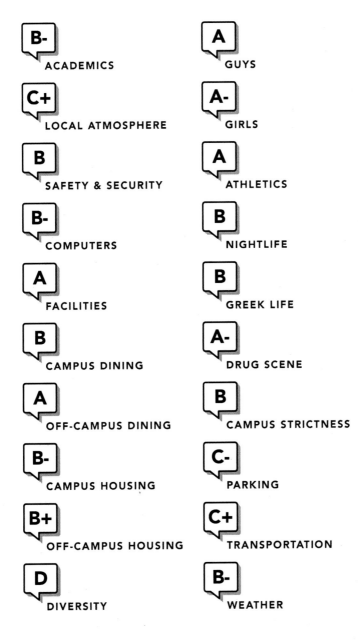

B- ACADEMICS

C+ LOCAL ATMOSPHERE

B SAFETY & SECURITY

B- COMPUTERS

A FACILITIES

B CAMPUS DINING

A OFF-CAMPUS DINING

B- CAMPUS HOUSING

B+ OFF-CAMPUS HOUSING

D DIVERSITY

A GUYS

A- GIRLS

A ATHLETICS

B NIGHTLIFE

B GREEK LIFE

A- DRUG SCENE

B CAMPUS STRICTNESS

C- PARKING

C+ TRANSPORTATION

B- WEATHER

Overall Experience

Students Speak Out On...
Overall Experience

"I've wanted to go to A&M since before I can remember. Everyone loves it. It's so different from any other place you'll ever visit. You will love it. I promise. Once an Aggie, always an Aggie."

"**This school is awesome**. The people here are so friendly and helpful. Everyday I am amazed at the dedication Aggies have for others. It's true that A&M has a bit of a conservative atmosphere, but there are plenty of liberal people as well. Don't get me wrong—just because it's a bit conservative, it doesn't mean we don't like to have a good time. You just have to find your niche. There are tons of things to get involved in."

Q "I just graduated from A&M, and it was **the best five years of my entire life**. You get out of college what you put in. My advice is to get involved in something on campus—be it Greek life, clubs, or something else. Make as many friends as possible. At a school of over 45,000 students, there wasn't a day that I walked around on campus and didn't see someone I knew."

Q "I kind of got lost in the mass of students. **Most people were very friendly**, but I think a smaller school would have been better for me."

Q "I love A&M for **its small-school feel on a big campus**. The tremendous school spirit makes you feel like you are a part of a huge family. I wish, in a way, that I would have gone out-of-state for a more challenging experience, in the realm of diversity at least."

Q "I love it. I can't see myself anywhere else but here. I'm an Aggie. Everyone is really nice and friendly. They always try to help you out, especially if it's your first year. It's a really nice campus. **Traditions are big, and they grow on you**—at least, they did on me, just like saying 'howdy.' Basically, I'm proud to say I'm an Aggie, and I bleed maroon! It's a part of me now."

Q "I did wish I was somewhere else. **I did not like the size of the school or the size of the classes**, and registering for classes is awful because there are over 45,000 students trying to do the same. You can never get the classes you want, which is why they do not expect you to graduate in four years."

Q "This is the best school ever. You will never find another school that is so friendly, has such school spirit, and is just **a huge family**. I love it here."

Q "My dad and grandpa both went here, and the strength of the traditions really attracted me to A&M. **The school is really consistent and stable**, and I like that."

Q "I would like to say that **I love Texas A&M**! Coming here has to be one of the best choices I ever made! If you decide to go here, you must go to Fish Camp. It's an awesome four days."

Q "A&M rules! It's the best school ever! There is **so much rich history**, great pride, and tradition."

Q "I think the traditions are stupid, and **too many people have their entire identity wrapped up in the school**. It's a neat place, but it shouldn't be your whole life."

Q "I have never wished I was anywhere else—I love it here. **There are lots of big cities within two hours**, so a road trip is always fun. You have to go to Austin if you make it down here. It's one of the coolest towns in the world."

Q "**I have so much pride in this school** and wouldn't go anywhere else. I don't think many other schools can boast such community as A&M."

Q "Texas A&M is awesome! I love my school; it's the greatest! We have tons of traditions, many unique to A&M, and some even honoring our fallen Aggies. **It's just an all around great school to go to**."

Q "**I love A&M**, and I really am glad to be here—it's lots of fun for everyone."

Q "I love A&M. **I've had a great experience so far**, and I wouldn't change it for the world."

Q "A&M has **the biggest network in the nation**. It is so easy to get jobs or get hooked up with other Aggies because we all share this pride in our school."

Q "I love A&M and wouldn't trade my experience here for anything. I think **most people who come here get really attached and hate to leave**. As they say, I bleed maroon. I've been here four years, and it has been a great time."

Q "I thought I hated it the whole first semester, but it turns out **you just have to find your place**—now, I love it."

Q "I went to A&M last year as a freshman, and I am not attending a second year because the school was not the right place for me. **It is very large and easy to get lost in the system**."

Q "**Being an Aggie is like being part of a family**, and I wouldn't change it for anything. Once an Aggie, always an Aggie! Going to the football games, baseball games, and basketball games is always fun, and you will have a great time. I am a little biased since I went to A&M, but I do recommend coming here. I have loved it here, and I can't praise it enough. There's nothing else like A&M!"

Q "It's like someone said, '**Looking in from the outside, you can't understand it**. Looking out from the inside, you can't explain it.' It holds true for me. I can't explain to you how much spirit there is, or how much I love A&M. I don't want to leave. I loved it, and A&M will always be my second home."

The College Prowler Take On...
Overall Experience

Most students either love or hate A&M, and those who hate it usually transfer out their first year. A&M offers an incredible educational and lifetime experience that most students thoroughly enjoy. If you have a problem with life at A&M, it's most likely because you haven't found a niche and you still feel lost in the crowd. In a school this big, it's not hard to feel as though you've vanished. It can be difficult to find people with common interests that you really click with, but if you get involved in student organizations and your classes, you'll figure it out. It can be intimidating at first, but don't give up. Going away to college is a big change, and it can take a while to get adjusted and find your place, no matter what kind of person you are.

Aggies have an overwhelming pride in their school, and the age-old traditions can seem annoying to a new student who has never been a part of them. However, the consistency of the traditions that carry on year after year offers a timeless experience that you can share with your any other A&M grad. Although times are constantly changing here, some things will always stay the same, and this gives A&M that special feeling that is hard to find at any other campus. Here, you are not just getting an education; you're becoming part of a whole new culture, taking part in its current events, and becoming part of its history. In the long run, A&M isn't just about going somewhere for four years to learn; It's like becoming part of a society that will continue to shape and mold your life, and the lives of those around you, forever.

The Inside Scoop

The Lowdown On...
The Inside Scoop

A&M Slang:

Know the slang, know the school. The following is a list of things you really need to know before coming to A&M. The more of these words you know, the better off you'll be.

The *Batt* - The *Battalion*, the student newspaper.
Boot Chaser - A girl who has the hots for a Corps guy.

Get off the field - What you'll yell if someone, other than the football players and the band, walks on Kyle field.
Get off the grass - What you'll hear if you walk on the MSC grass.
Get off the wood - What you'll hear when you sing the fight song. It means get off the benches that you're standing on during football games.
Howdy - Hello.

→

→

Mugging - What you do when the lights go out on Kyle Field, otherwise known as kissing.

Non-Reg - Someone not in the Corps.

Reg - Someone in the Corps of Cadets.

Rev - Reveille, the mascot Border Collie.

Scho-Pro - Short for Scholastic Probation.

Sweet E's - Sweet Eugene's, a popular coffee hangout.

T.U. - Our rival school, the University of Texas.

Two Percenter - Students who don't participate in A&M traditions.

Uncover - Take off your hat.

Things I Wish I Knew Before Coming to A&M

• Most people don't dress up to go to class.

• No one carries her purse to class.

• If you're driving to class, leave at least one hour early to get parking.

• Remember to bring a Scantron to class on test days.

• Join an organization to make the school feel smaller.

• Only join one or two organizations. It's not like high school, where you can do everything and still make good grades.

• Don't park under trees. There is a disgustingly large bird population.

Tips to Succeed at A&M

- Take "Succeeding in College" your first semester.

- Check out the professors before you register for classes.

- Have frequent meetings with your advisor regarding your academic plan.

- Have frequent meetings with your professors so you can get good recommendations on your resume.

A&M Urban Legends

Our mascot attends class with the Corps guy that keeps him, and it's been said that if Reveille barks during your class, then class is dismissed.

Traditions

12th Man
Students stand at every football game in honor of E. King Gill, who was called out of the stands to play for the Aggies in 1922. Since most of the team was injured, Gill suited up and stood ready to play for the rest of the game if his team needed him. Although he never played, students now stand for the entire game to show that the 11 men on the gridiron can call on them any time for help.

Ring Dance
The college version of Senior Prom

Boot Dance
The college version of Junior Prom

Midnight Yell

At midnight before every home football game, Aggies gather at Kyle Field for yell practice. Bring a date, because when the lights go out, you kiss.

Every time the Aggies score, you score

At a football game, if the team scores a point, you kiss your date.

Aggie Ring

When you have completed 96 credit hours, you get to order your ring, which is the same for every graduate, except for the class year. Since everyone gets the same ring design year after year, this creates a historical bond between Aggies. In the end, this makes A&M graduates unmistakably recognizable to one another.

Muster

Every April 21st, Muster brings Aggies together worldwide to honor the passing of Aggies that year and celebrate their memory. Candles are lit in their honor, and a roll-call is spoken with their comrade answering "here" in their place.

Silver Taps

If an A&M student dies, a tribute is held in the Academic Plaza on the first Tuesday of the month. A ceremonial march-in by the Ross Volunteers is followed by a 21-gun salute and the playing of taps three times from the dome of the Academic Building, facing to the north, the south, and the west. It is not played to the east, because the sun will never rise on that Aggie again.

Finding a Job or Internship

The Lowdown On...
Finding a Job or Internship

Attend career fairs for your college or department in the spring to look for internships and full-time employment. Register at the Career Center for a nominal fee to get help finding a job your graduation semester.

Advice

Look for an internship the summer after your sophomore or junior year. This makes getting a job much easier. Employers are always looking to make sure that you have on the job experience, and internships are the best way to do this while still in school.

Career Center Resources & Services

The Career Center is located on the second floor of Koldus. For more information, go to their Web site at *http://careercenter.tamu.edu.* Their services include:

Resume Writing

Internships

Dining Etiquette

Interviewing Skills

Career Fairs

Online Assessments

Career Advising

Average Salary Information

Below is a list of the average starting salaries for Aggies graduating with specialized degrees:

Accounting	$42,307
Aerospace Engineering	$56,167
Agricultural Business	$31,000
Agricultural Development	$35,375
Agricultural Economics	$35,000
Agricultural Journalism	$22,000
Agricultural Management	$45,000
Animal Science	$30,000
Bioenvironmental Science	$32,000
Civil Engineering	$39,942
Computer Engineering	$49,905
Construction Science	$42,603
Economics	$37,170
Education	$35,000
Electrical Engineering	$62,131
Elementary Education	$42,700

English	$36,800
Engineering	$45,000
Environmental Design	$35,160
Food Science and Technology	$32,833
Genetics	$25,000
Health	$27,855
History	$34,554
Interdisciplinary Studies	$33,079
Interdisciplinary Technology	$37,000
Kinesiology	$31,625
Landscape Architecture	$33,500
Microbiology	$29,225
Molecular and Cell Biology	$23,000
Nutritional Sciences	$21,333
Plant and Soil Sciences	$37,000
Psychology	$32,044
Rangeland Ecology	$29,333
Recreation and Tourism Science	$32,165
Speech Communication	$35,587
Veterinary Medicine	$25,365
Wildlife Fisheries Science	$26,000

Firms That Frequently Hire Graduates

Accenture, AXA Advisors, Chevron Texaco, CIA, Cintas, Dell, Deloitte/Touche, Enterprise Rent-a-car, Ernst/Young, Excel, Exxon Mobil, Ferguson, FMC, GE, Halff Assc, Halliburton, HEB, Jones/Carter, KPMG, LJA Engr, Lockheed Martin, Northwestern Mutual, PWC, Raytheon, Royce Homes, Ryan & Co, Schlumberger, Shell, TAMU, Target, Texas Instruments, the Boeing Co, Univ Computer Systems, Walgreens

Alumni

The Lowdown On...
Alumni

Web Site:
www.aggienetwork.com

Office:
Association of Former Students
505 George Bush Drive
College Station, TX 77840-2918
(979) 845-7514
afs@aggienetwork.com

Alumni Center:
The Clayton W. Williams Jr. Alumni Center is home to the Association of Former Students. The Alumni Center offers a place for A&M meetings, receptions, luncheons, and lectures.

Services Available:
Aggie Ring (for current students), A&M Clubs, Reunions, Leadership Council, Aggie Muster, Annual Giving, Bridal Portraits, Texas Aggie Magazine, Travel Programs

Major Alumni Events

Most major events center around the football games, like home tailgating parties, but another important alumni event at A&M is Muster. Muster is held on April 21st every year, and there are ceremonies at A&M, as well as in cities across the globe. Muster began as a celebration of Texas's Independence on San Jacinto Day, but has evolved into a celebration of the lives of the Aggies that died during the past year. Every year, the ceremony is dedicated to the class that graduated 50 years earlier. All alumni are invited back to campus for tours and the Camaraderie Barbeque. That night, some poetry is read, followed by the Roll Call for the Absent. The name of every Aggie that died during that past year is read, and a family member or friend says "here" for the Aggie they knew that passed away. This is a way of showing that the person is still with them as part of the Aggie Spirit.

Alumni Publications

Texas Aggie Magazine

This publication comes out every other month and is free to active alumni.

Did You Know?

Famous TAMU Alumni

Chuck Knoblauch (1989) - Former Major League Baseball player

Lyle Lovett (1982) - Famous singer, was married to Julia Roberts

Rick Perry (1972) - Governor of Texas

Student Organizations

A&M offers over 700 student organizations in various categories. Here are some examples:

Academic

Texas A&M Architectural League

Beta Alpha Psi

Business Administration Society

African-American Business Society/National Association of Black Accountants

American Society of Agricultural Engineers

ASM International

Liberal Arts Student Council

George Bush School Student Government Association

Academic-Professional

Society of Professional Journalists

TAMSA organization for Minority Issues in Medicine

TAMSA-Psychiatry Interest Group

TAMSA Class of 2004

TAMSA Family Medicine Interest Group

TAMSA Women in Medicine

Campus Service

Aggie Fish Club

Aggie Orientation Leader Program

Committee Reaching Every Woman

(Campus Service continued)

Fish Camp

Freshmen Leaders in Progress

Howdy Camp

Maggies

Transfer Ags

YARMY

Cultural/International

African American Student Coalition

A&M International Fellowship

Aggie Friends of Israel

Asian-American Association

Bangladesh Student Association

China Club

Hellenic Student Association

International Graduate Student Association

International Student Association

Texas A&M Thai Student Association

Whoopstock Council

Performing and Visual Arts

Aggie Swamp Club

Aggie Wranglers

Century Singers

Dance Arts Society

Freudian Slip Improvisational Comedy Troupe

Percussion Studio

University Symphonic Band

Texas A&M University Singing Cadets

Women's Chorus

Yemanja: Drums of Passion

Religious

Aggie Sisters for Christ

Asian American Christian Fellowship

Baptist Student Ministry

Beta Upsilon Chi (Brothers Under Christ)

Breakaway

Brotherhood of Christian Aggies

Fellowship of Christian Brothers

Doulos

I.G.N.I.T.E. Ministries

Impact

Upstream

Yada

Spirit and Tradition

Aggie Angels

Aggie Hostess

Diamond Darlings

Bonfire Coalition for Students

Reed Rowdies

Texas Aggie Yell Leaders

Student Government

Aggie Muster Committee

CARPOOL (Caring Aggies R Protecting Over Our Lives)

SGA - Student Senate

SGA Replant

The Big Event

Traditions Council

The Best & Worst

The Ten BEST Things About A&M

1 Traditions

2 Unity

3 Chivalry

4 Respect for history

5 Freebirds

6 Northgate

7 Football

8 School spirit

9 The business school

10 The Aggie network

The Ten WORST Things About A&M

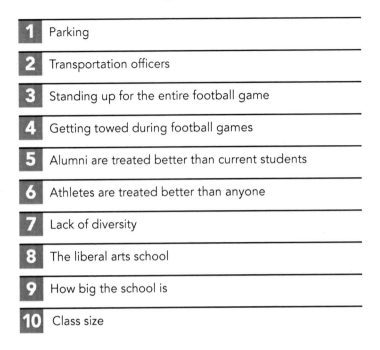

1 Parking

2 Transportation officers

3 Standing up for the entire football game

4 Getting towed during football games

5 Alumni are treated better than current students

6 Athletes are treated better than anyone

7 Lack of diversity

8 The liberal arts school

9 How big the school is

10 Class size

Visiting

The Lowdown On...
Visiting

Hotel Information:

Aggieland Kiva Inn
104 Texas Avenue
College Station, TX 77840
(979) 846-7333
www.aggielandkiva.com
Distance from Campus:
1 block
Price Range: $59–$89

Best Western at Chimney Hill
901 E. Universtiy Drive
College Station, TX 77840
(979) 260-9150
www.bestwestern.com
Distance from Campus:
1.8 miles
Price Range: $68–$74

➜

Courtyard Marriot

3939 State Highway 6
South College Station, TX
77845
(979) 695-8111
www.marriott.com
Distance from Campus:
4.3 miles
Price Range: $79–$94

Hampton Inn

320 Texas Avenue South
A College Station, TX 77840
(979) 846-0184
http://college-station-tx-
us.hotels-x.net/Hampton-inn-
college-station.html
Distance from Campus:
0.1 miles
Price Range: $84

Hilton College Station and Conference Center

801 University Drive East
College Station, TX
77840-2116
(979) 693-7500
www.hilton.com
Distance from Campus:
2.2 miles
Price Range: $119–$124

Holiday Inn Express

1203 University Drive East
College Station, TX 77840
(979) 846-8700
www.pricerighthotels.com
Distance from Campus:
1.6 miles
Price Range: $69–$79

Motel 6

2327 Texas Avenue South
College Station, TX 77840
(979) 696-3379
www.motel6.com
Distance from Campus:
1.9 miles
Price Range: $35–$39

Ramada Inn

1502 Texas Ave.
College Station, TX 77840
(979) 693-9891
www.ramada.com
Distance from Campus:
1.2 miles
Price Range: $47–$60

Take a Campus Virtual Tour

http://communications.tamu.edu/visitors/virtual-campus.shtml

To Schedule a Group Information Session or Interview

Call the Visitor Center at (979) 845-5851 to schedule an appointment and get more information. You can also e-mail them at vis-cntr@tamu.edu.

Campus Tours

Call the Visitor Center at (979) 845-5851 at least two weeks before you would like to visit to schedule an appointment. Tours are not held on weekends, but are held several times a day during each weekday. The exact times vary depending on the time of year, but to check out when tours are running in the next couple months, go to *http://communications.tamu. edu/visitors/walking-tours.shtml.*

Overnight Visits

The only overnight visit the school offers is "Spend the Night with the Corps," a program for students interested in joining the Corps of Cadets. In this program, the prospective students get to participate in all Corps activities, sleep in the Corps dorm, go to an application workshop and experience college life. For more information, or to sign up for the program, go to *http://www.aggiecorps.org/home/prospective/stn.*

Directions to Campus

Driving from the North:
- Take I45 South to Madisonville.
- Go South/West on Highway 21.
- Go south on Highway 6 through Bryan.
- Take the University exit, campus is on the left.

Driving from the South:
- Take Highway 290 east to Highway 6 north.
- Highway 6 turns into Texas Avenue.
- Turn Left on George Bush Drive, campus in on the right.

Driving from the East:
- Take Highway 21 South/West to Highway 6.
- Merge onto 6 South.
- Take the University exit, campus is on the left.

Driving from the West:
- Take 21 North/East to Highway 6.
- Take 6 South.
- Take the University exit, campus is on the left.

Words to Know

Academic Probation – A suspension imposed on a student if he or she fails to keep up with the school's minimum academic requirements. Those unable to improve their grades after receiving this warning can face dismissal.

Beer Pong / Beirut – A drinking game involving cups of beer arranged in a pyramid shape on each side of a table. The goal is to get a ping pong ball into one of the opponent's cups by throwing the ball or hitting it with a paddle. If the ball lands in a cup, the opponent is required to drink the beer.

Bid – An invitation from a fraternity or sorority to 'pledge' (join) that specific house.

Blue-Light Phone – Brightly-colored phone posts with a blue light bulb on top. These phones exist for security purposes and are located at various outside locations around most campuses. In an emergency, a student can pick up one of these phones (free of charge) to connect with campus police or a security escort.

Campus Police – Police who are specifically assigned to a given institution. Campus police are typically not regular city officers; they are employed by the university in a full-time capacity.

Club Sports – A level of sports that falls somewhere between varsity and intramural. If a student is unable to commit to a varsity team but has a lot of passion for athletics, a club sport could be a better, less intense option. Even less demanding, intramural (IM) sports often involve no traveling and considerably less time.

Cocaine – An illegal drug. Also known as "coke" or "blow," cocaine often resembles a white crystalline or powdery substance. It is highly addictive and dangerous.

Common Application – An application with which students can apply to multiple schools.

Course Registration – The period of official class selection for the upcoming quarter or semester. Prior to registration, it is best to prepare several back-up courses in case a particular class becomes full. If a course is full, students can place themselves on the waitlist, although this still does not guarantee entry.

Division Athletics – Athletic classifications range from Division I to Division III. Division IA is the most competitive, while Division III is considered to be the least competitive.

Dorm – A dorm (or dormitory) is an on-campus housing facility. Dorms can provide a range of options from suite-style rooms to more communal options that include shared bathrooms. Most first-year students live in dorms. Some upperclassmen who wish to stay on campus also choose this option.

Early Action – An application option with which a student can apply to a school and receive an early acceptance response without a binding commitment. This system is becoming less and less available.

Early Decision – An application option that students should use only if they are certain they plan to attend the school in question. If a student applies using the early decision option and is admitted, he or she is required and bound to attend that university. Admission rates are usually higher among students who apply through early decision, as the student is clearly indicating that the school is his or her first choice.

Ecstasy – An illegal drug. Also known as "E" or "X," ecstasy looks like a pill and most resembles an aspirin. Considered a party drug, ecstasy is very dangerous and can be deadly.

Ethernet – An extremely fast Internet connection available in most university-owned residence halls. To use an Ethernet connection properly, a student will need a network card and cable for his or her computer.

Fake ID – A counterfeit identification card that contains false information. Most commonly, students get fake IDs with altered birthdates so that they appear to be older than 21 (and therefore of legal drinking age). Even though it is illegal, many college students have fake IDs in hopes of purchasing alcohol or getting into bars.

Frosh – Slang for "freshman" or "freshmen."

Hazing – Initiation rituals administered by some fraternities or sororities as part of the pledging process. Many universities have outlawed hazing due to its degrading and sometimes dangerous nature.

Intramurals (IMs) – A popular, and usually free, sport league in which students create teams and compete against one another. These sports vary in competitiveness and can include a range of activities—everything from billiards to water polo. IM sports are a great way to meet people with similar interests.

Keg – Officially called a half-barrel, a keg contains roughly 200 12-ounce servings of beer.

LSD – An illegal drug. Also known as acid, this hallucinogenic drug most commonly resembles a tab of paper.

Marijuana – An illegal drug. Also known as weed or pot; along with alcohol, marijuana is one of the most commonly-found drugs on campuses across the country.

Major –The focal point of a student's college studies; a specific topic that is studied for a degree. Examples of majors include physics, English, history, computer science, economics, business, and music. Many students decide on a specific major before arriving on campus, while others are simply "undecided" until delcaring a major. Those who are extremely interested in two areas can also choose to double major.

Meal Block – The equivalent of one meal. Students on a meal plan usually receive a fixed number of meals per week. Each meal, or "block," can be redeemed at the school's dining facilities in place of cash. Often, a student's weekly allotment of meal blocks will be forfeited if not used.

Minor – An additional focal point in a student's education. Often serving as a complement or addition to a student's main area of focus, a minor has fewer requirements and prerequisites to fulfill than a major. Minors are not required for graduation from most schools; however some students who want to explore many different interests choose to pursue both a major and a minor.

Mushrooms – An illegal drug. Also known as "shrooms," this drug resembles regular mushrooms but is extremely hallucinogenic.

Off-Campus Housing – Housing from a particular landlord or rental group that is not affiliated with the university. Depending on the college, off-campus housing can range from extremely popular to non-existent. Students who choose to live off campus are typically given more freedom, but they also have to deal with possible subletting scenarios, furniture, bills, and other issues. In addition to these factors, rental prices and distance often affect a student's decision to move off campus.

Office Hours – Time that teachers set aside for students who have questions about coursework. Office hours are a good forum for students to go over any problems and to show interest in the subject material.

Pledging – The early phase of joining a fraternity or sorority, pledging takes place after a student has gone through rushand received a bid. Pledging usually lasts between one and two semesters. Once the pledging period is complete and a particular student has done everything that is required to become a member, that student is considered a brother or sister. If a fraternity or a sorority would decide to "haze" a group of students, this initiation would take place during the pledging period.

Private Institution – A school that does not use tax revenue to subsidize education costs. Private schools typically cost more than public schools and are usually smaller.

Prof – Slang for "professor."

Public Institution – A school that uses tax revenue to subsidize education costs. Public schools are often a good value for in-state residents and tend to be larger than most private colleges.

Quarter System (or Trimester System) – A type of academic calendar system. In this setup, students take classes for three academic periods. The first quarter usually starts in late September or early October and concludes right before Christmas. The second quarter usually starts around early to mid–January and finishes up around March or April. The last quarter, or "third quarter," usually starts in late March or early April and finishes up in late May or Mid-June. The fourth quarter is summer. The major difference between the quarter system and semester system is that students take more, less comprehensive courses under the quarter calendar.

RA (Resident Assistant) – A student leader who is assigned to a particular floor in a dormitory in order to help to the other students who live there. An RA's duties include ensuring student safety and providing assistance wherever possible.

Recitation – An extension of a specific course; a review session. Some classes, particularly large lectures, are supplemented with mandatory recitation sessions that provide a relatively personal class setting.

Rolling Admissions – A form of admissions. Most commonly found at public institutions, schools with this type of policy continue to accept students throughout the year until their class sizes are met. For example, some schools begin accepting students as early as December and will continue to do so until April or May.

Room and Board – This figure is typically the combined cost of a university-owned room and a meal plan.

Room Draw/Housing Lottery – A common way to pick on-campus room assignments for the following year. If a student decides to remain in university-owned housing, he or she is assigned a unique number that, along with seniority, is used to determine his or her housing for the next year.

Rush – The period in which students can meet the brothers and sisters of a particular chapter and find out if a given fraternity or sorority is right for them. Rushing a fraternity or a sorority is not a requirement at any school. The goal of rush is to give students who are serious about pledging a feel for what to expect.

Semester System – The most common type of academic calendar system at college campuses. This setup typically includes two semesters in a given school year. The fall semester starts around the end of August or early September and concludes before winter vacation. The spring semester usually starts in mid-January and ends in late April or May.

Student Center/Rec Center/Student Union – A common area on campus that often contains study areas, recreation facilities, and eateries. This building is often a good place to meet up with fellow students; depending on the school, the student center can have a huge role or a non-existent role in campus life.

Student ID – A university-issued photo ID that serves as a student's key to school-related functions. Some schools require students to show these cards in order to get into dorms, libraries, cafeterias, and other facilities. In addition to storing meal plan information, in some cases, a student ID can actually work as a debit card and allow students to purchase things from bookstores or local shops.

Suite – A type of dorm room. Unlike dorms that feature communal bathrooms shared by the entire floor, suites offer bathrooms shared only among the suite. Suite-style dorm rooms can house anywhere from two to ten students.

TA (Teacher's Assistant) – An undergraduate or grad student who helps in some manner with a specific course. In some cases, a TA will teach a class, assist a professor, grade assignments, or conduct office hours.

Undergraduate – A student in the process of studying for his or her bachelor's degree.

ABOUT THE AUTHOR

I would like to thank the Academy for believing in me enough to give me this opportunity—just kidding. Writing this book has been a blast, and I hope you've had just as much fun reading it.

I graduated from the fine university of Texas A&M with a journalism major. I call it a commemorative diploma. I hope to continue my passion for writing for the rest of my life.

Thanks to the College Prowler staff for all their support and patience. They believe in this book so much, and it was an honor to be part of it.

Thanks for buying this book and reading it! Good luck in your college endeavors. If you have any questions, e-mail me. If you have any compliments, e-mail me. If you have any complaints, e-mail Luke.

Sincerely,

Ashley Marshall

Ashleymarshall@collegeprowler.com

Notes

Notes

....

....

....

....

....

....

....

....

....

....

....

....

....

Notes

....

....

....

....

....

....

....

....

....

....

....

....

....

Notes

....

....

....

....

....

....

....

....

....

....

....

....

....

....

Notes

....

....

....

....

....

....

....

....

....

....

....

....

....

Notes

....

....

....

....

....

....

....

....

....

....

....

....

....

Notes

....

....

....

....

....

....

....

....

....

....

....

....

....

Notes

....

....

....

....

....

....

....

....

....

....

....

....

....

Notes

....

....

....

....

....

....

....

....

....

....

....

....

....

....

Notes

....

....

....

....

....

....

....

....

....

....

....

....

....

Notes

....

....

....

....

....

....

....

....

....

....

....

....

....

Notes

....

....

....

....

....

....

....

....

....

....

....

....

....

Notes

....

....

....

....

....

....

....

....

....

....

....

....

....

....

Notes

....

....

....

....

....

....

....

....

....

....

....

....

....

Notes

....

....

....

....

....

....

....

....

....

....

....

....

....

....

Notes

....

....

....

....

....

....

....

....

....

....

....

....

....

Notes

....

....

....

....

....

....

....

....

....

....

....

....

....

Notes

....

....

....

....

....

....

....

....

....

....

....

....

....

Notes

....

....

....

....

....

....

....

....

....

....

....

....

....

Notes

....

....

....

....

....

....

....

....

....

....

....

....

....

Notes

....

....

....

....

....

....

....

....

....

....

....

....

....

Notes

....

....

....

....

....

....

....

....

....

....

....

....

....

Notes

Notes

....
....
....
....
....
....
....
....
....
....
....
....
....

California Colleges

California dreamin'?
This book is a must have for you!

CALIFORNIA COLLEGES
7¼" X 10", 762 Pages Paperback
$29.95 Retail
1-59658-501-3

Stanford, UC Berkeley, Caltech—California is home
to some of America's greatest institutes of higher
learning. *California Colleges* gives the lowdown on 24
of the best, side by side, in one prodigious volume.

New England Colleges

Looking for peace in the Northeast?
Pick up this regional guide to New England!

NEW ENGLAND COLLEGES
7¼" X 10", 1015 Pages Paperback
$29.95 Retail
1-59658-504-8

New England is the birthplace of many prestigious
universities, and with so many to choose from, picking
the right school can be a tough decision. With inside
information on over 34 competive Northeastern
schools, *New England Colleges* provides the same
high-quality information prospective students expect
from College Prowler in one all-inclusive,
easy-to-use reference.

Schools of the South

Headin' down south? This book will help you find your way to the perfect school!

SCHOOLS OF THE SOUTH
7¼" X 10", 773 Pages Paperback
$29.95 Retail
1-59658-503-X

Southern pride is always strong. Whether it's across town or across state, many Southern students are devoted to their home sweet home. *Schools of the South* offers an honest student perspective on 36 universities available south of the Mason-Dixon.

Untangling the Ivy League

The ultimate book for everything Ivy!

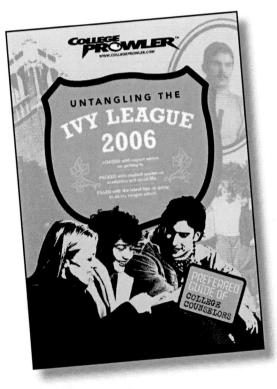

UNTANGLING THE IVY LEAGUE
7¼" X 10", 567 Pages Paperback
$24.95 Retail
1-59658-500-5

Ivy League students, alumni, admissions officers, and other top insiders get together to tell it like it is. *Untangling the Ivy League* covers every aspect—from admissions and athletics to secret societies and urban legends—of the nation's eight oldest, wealthiest, and most competitive colleges and universities.

Need Help Paying For School?

Apply for our scholarship!

College Prowler awards thousands of dollars a year to students who compose the best essays. E-mail scholarship@collegeprowler.com for more information, or call 1-800-290-2682.

Apply now at ***www.collegeprowler.com***

Tell Us What Life Is Really Like at Your School!

Have you ever wanted to let people know what your college is really like? Now's your chance to help millions of high school students choose the right college.

Let your voice be heard.

Check out *www.collegeprowler.com* for more info!

Need More Help?

Do you have more questions about this school?
Can't find a certain statistic? College Prowler is
here to help. We are the best source of college
information out there. We have a network
of thousands of students who can get the latest
information on any school to you ASAP.
E-mail us at info@collegeprowler.com with your
college-related questions.

E-Mail Us Your College-Related Questions!

Check out *www.collegeprowler.com* for more details.
1-800-290-2682

Write For Us!

Get published! Voice your opinion.

Writing a College Prowler guidebook is both fun and rewarding; our open-ended format allows your own creativity free reign. Our writers have been featured in national newspapers and have seen their names in bookstores across the country. Now is your chance to break into the publishing industry with one of the country's fastest-growing publishers!

Apply now at ***www.collegeprowler.com***

Contact editor@collegeprowler.com or call 1-800-290-2682 for more details.

Pros and Cons

Still can't figure out if this is the right school for you?
You've already read through this in-depth guide; why not
list the pros and cons? It will really help with narrowing down
your decision and determining whether or not
this school is right for you.

Pros	Cons
....	....
....	....
....	....
....	....
....	....
....	....
....	....
....	....
....	....
....	....
....	....
....	....
....	....

Pros and Cons

Still can't figure out if this is the right school for you?
You've already read through this in-depth guide; why not
list the pros and cons? It will really help with narrowing down
your decision and determining whether or not
this school is right for you.

Pros	Cons
....	....
....	....
....	....
....	....
....	....
....	....
....	....
....	....
....	....
....	....
....	....
....	....
....	....